SERVING

A NOW

GOD

Pete Martin

ISBN 979-8-88851-614-0 (Paperback)
ISBN 979-8-88851-615-7 (Digital)

Covenant Books
11661 Hwy 707
Murrells Inlet, SC 29576
www.covenantbooks.com

CONTENTS

Introduction v

Chapter 1:   The Battle 1
Chapter 2:   A Place Called Eden 6
Chapter 3:   The Time Trap 12
Chapter 4:   Stressed Out 17
Chapter 5:   Life Abundant 23
Chapter 6:   The Struggle 30
Chapter 7:   Pushing through the Pain 36
Chapter 8:   It's All about Me 43
Chapter 9:   Battle Gear 51
Chapter 10: Love Conquers All 57
Chapter 11: Can You Hear Me? 63
Chapter 12: Faith Walk 69
Chapter 13: Religion Is Not Relationship 74
Chapter 14: Put It into Practice 80
Chapter 15: The Temple 86
Chapter 16: Holy Spirit Power 93
Chapter 17: The Power of the Blood 100
Chapter 18: Death Is Not the End 106
Chapter 19: Community 111
Chapter 20: Power of the Tongue 116
Chapter 21: He Is Coming Back 122
Chapter 22: The Homecoming 128

INTRODUCTION

In modern churches today, some pastors preach sermons depicting the Christian walk as a trouble-free life blessed with material possessions. Many people have false conversions based on this information and soon fall away from the faith when the above promise is not fulfilled. This multitude then spreads their testimony of discontent to others, a poison driving people away from God instead of toward Him.

If you are not a Christian or are new in the faith, you may be confused about exactly what it means to live as a believer of the Lord Jesus Christ. This book will illustrate what the life of a true Christian should be like and the biblical promises for those who followed Jesus. Serving God in today's culture is not an easy job, and it is not always going to bring you *happiness*. The message of Jesus is not in alignment with what the world's culture esteems but depicts godly wisdom on how people should conduct their lives.

The truth is God loves you and wants the very best for you. He will fill your existence with peace and joy through His Son, Jesus. And when does God want you to have this tranquility? The Bible states, "Now is the time of God's favor, now is the day of salvation" (2 Corinthians 6:2). God wants you to have this covenant lifestyle today—right now!

Come explore the start of humanity and how the world transitioned into the state it is in today. Learn about your very real enemy, Satan, and how he wants to wreak havoc in your life with the intention of destroying you. Discover how the God of the universe devised a plan to save us from destruction and give us hope and a future. Experience what life could be like Serving a Now God.

CHAPTER 1

The Battle

The alarm clock disrupts your slumber with its annoying urgency. The business of the pending day floods your mind swiftly, chasing away your peace. You moan and sink deeper into your covers, as if they were a shield against reality. The faint smell of brewing coffee is the only friendly invitation to the new morning. You drag yourself out of the bed to greet the start of another day.

Have you ever wondered why you are living this life? You try to figure out the purpose of this everyday existence as you pencil off another day on the calendar, waiting for the weekend or the next big vacation. In the meantime, your daily diversions may be your next cigarette or a night out at the neighborhood bar. These are the crutches that make life bearable as you wait for that special person to come into your life or the new job that will finally make you happy. Sadly, happiness is only a fleeting glimpse, an illusion that never seems to appear.

For many people today, the consistent pressure of day-to-day activities creates stress that makes their life less enjoyable. There never seems to be enough time to get everything done. The paycheck can never be stretched far enough to cover all the bills. Life always throws you a curveball at the most inopportune time, and you feel like you are always a day late and a dollar short. Life can sometimes seem like one big discouragement of never-ending problems without solutions that keep you pondering, "When will all of these problems end?"

Your existence was not meant to be a time void of joy and peace. It was meant to be the gateway to an eternal relationship with the one true God, a God who wants to fill your time here on earth with an abundance of peace and joy that transcends all understanding. When does God want you to have this peace and joy? Now, this very moment!

You may ask, "If God exists and loves me so much, then why is my life in such shambles?" Why is everything in chaos without a clear path to sanity? For the most part, we are the creators of our own problems. Every decision we make delivers some kind of result. If you make good decisions, you usually get a positive result. The problem is most of us are making bad choices that can lead to a lot of heartache and misery. To compound the problem, if one bad decision after another is made, a person's life can end up being a mess very quickly. This principle is outlined in the Bible, and it is called *reaping* and *sowing* (Galatians 6:7).

Whatever seed (decision) you plant will determine what kind of harvest you will have. Just like you cannot plant a tomato seed and get a pear, you cannot make a poor choice and expect a great outcome. Examine some of the choices you have made recently. Were they sound decisions that brought a valued outcome or poor ones that only produced bigger problems? Change the way you think and you can change the path of your life. Now most people understand if you habitually smoke tobacco, drink alcohol in excess, or overeat, these decisions will probably lead to health problems later in life. If you smoke cigarettes all your life and you contract lung cancer, the cause of your condition is quite obvious.

But some of you may be thinking, *I make fairly good decisions, but my life is still a mess.* This does not mean the principle of reaping and sowing mentioned in the paragraph above is invalid, because anything that happens to you is caused by something whether you are aware of what that reason is or not. I am sure in the Bible story of Job, the main character was probably wondering the same thing. Job was a righteous and upright man who was faithful to God, but one day his life began to rapidly fall apart. He lost his livestock, his children, and then finally his health failed him. Job was perplexed why this was happening to him, but what he did not realize was a demonic influence was wreaking havoc in his life. Even though Job was ignorant of this information, the effects of this meddling sure disrupted his day. Could this happen to you? To answer this question, you must first know who you are. You are God's creation, and He made you in His image. Since you are God's creation, you have a very real enemy who hates God and is out to destroy you. This enemy is the same one who attacked Job, and his name is the devil or Satan.

You may have thought the devil was a fictional character, like the type depicted by the media, a man dressed in a red jumpsuit displaying pointed ears, a long tail, sporting a pitchfork. The devil would like you to continue to believe he is not real. If you believe he does not exist, he can continue to disrupt your life without your even raising a finger to stop him. The truth is Satan is real and alive on the earth today, ready to tempt you to make bad choices. He will entice you to take the easiest path with the promise of instant gratification. Those who have wisdom will realize there is no free ride, and the easy path is usually a trail to destruction. Even if the devil cannot tempt you to make bad decisions, he will try his best to discourage you and make your life miserable.

So where did the devil come from? God created the devil and named him Lucifer, meaning "light bearer." You may be thinking why God would create a being who attacks mankind and causes humanity such pain. When God first created Lucifer, he was a powerful and beautiful cherub (type of angel) who sat in His presence. He was created to be a perfect servant of God and was without flaw or blemish (Ezekiel 28:14). So what happened to Lucifer that caused him to shift from good to evil? Lucifer rebelled against God as he tried to elevate himself to be the same as God. This action of rebellion or disobedience toward God is called sin, a serious condition that separates the sinner from God. The created being saw himself as being equal to the Creator. This rebellion against God is a form of pride that is illustrated in these verses from Isaiah:

> How you are fallen from heaven, O Lucifer, son of the morning! How you are cut down to the ground, you who weakened the nations!
>
> For you said in your heart: I will ascend into heaven, I will exalt my throne above the star of God; I will also sit on the mount of the congregation on the farthest sides of the north;
>
> I will ascend above the heights of the clouds; I will be like the Most High. (Isaiah 14:12–14)

This act of pride resulted in Lucifer's being kicked out of heaven with a third of the angels who joined with him in this act of rebellion (Revelation 12:9). Lucifer and his followers were cast down to earth, where they reside today.

With this transition, Lucifer was given a new name, Satan, which in Hebrew means *adversary*. This is a description of what Lucifer had become, an enemy of God in opposition to the truth. Another popular name for Satan is the devil, which is Greek for *slanderer*. The devil is looking to wreak destruction by spreading his lies, and the Bible cautions us to be on the lookout for him. First Peter 5:8 states, "Be sober, be vigilant, because your adversary the devil walks about like a roaring lion seeking who he may devour," and the devil is looking to devour you.

What is the devil's mission? "To kill, steal and destroy" (John 10:10), and you are his target. Satan wants to kill your hopes, steal your joy, and totally destroy your life. He wants to do this to keep your focus off the One who wants you to have a better, more abundant life, the Lord Jesus Christ. If all you have faced in your life is struggle, pain, and lack, you are experiencing exactly what Satan wants you to feel. Satan wants you to walk through life wearing spiritual blinders that prevent you from seeing any glimpse of hope. Satan does this knowing if you die without a relationship with God, you will die not only a physical death but also a spiritual death. This spiritual death is an eternal separation from God. Not only is this a problem in the afterlife, but it also affects your present condition by keeping you from the abundant peace and happiness you could possess now. Jesus wants to remove those spiritual blinders and show you the right path for your existence.

The devil is a great deceiver, and he can successfully keep you spiritually unaware of the ways of God. Most people have lived their whole life in deception and do not even realize they are in bondage. The key to freedom is Jesus, Who has given you a free gift to break the chains of evil. Although the devil is very crafty and has many ways to keep you disillusioned, Jesus can lift this fog of evil if you trust in Him and accept salvation. The weapons of righteousness can combat anything Satan can conjure up. This war is being conducted in the spiritual realm, and you are guaranteed victory if you have Jesus on your side. Living life without Jesus will lead to your demise in this life and the next. This does not mean when you accept Jesus as your Savior that your life will be problem-free, but there will always be hope and strength in the middle of the storm.

This book will take a closer look at the strategies Satan uses to try to deceive us in order to separate people from the one true God. We will examine how we can combat the devil in this spiritual war and live a God-filled life that is victorious while helping others to do the same. But first, let's look at where man's battle first began, a place called Eden.

CHAPTER 2

A Place Called Eden

> The Lord God planted a garden eastward on Eden, and there
> He put the man whom He had formed. And out of the ground
> the Lord God made every tree grow that is pleasant to the sight
> and good for food. The tree of life was also in the midst of
> the garden and the tree of the knowledge of good and evil.
> —Genesis 2:8–9

God created man from the dust of the earth and placed him into the Garden of Eden. In the garden was everything man needed to sustain himself. The garden was a place of beauty, not tainted with the pollution and decay like the world is experiencing in this present age. The provision of God can be seen throughout the garden: four rivers supplying life-giving water to an abundance of different trees that supplied a variety of delicious fruit. The temperature in the garden must have been pleasant for Adam to have walked unclothed in the garden. A perfect God created a perfect garden that even had valuable commodities like gold and gemstones located on the property (Genesis 2:8–12). It was an absolute paradise.

God was greatly concerned with Adam's welfare, for He loved His creation wholeheartedly. So when God saw Adam was lonely, He made a companion for him and created a woman. God gave Adam free rein in the garden with one stipulation: not to eat from the tree of the knowledge of good and evil. It was God's desire for Adam to live in the garden and fellowship with Him for eternity, but something changed that.

> Now the serpent was more cunning than any beast of the field which the Lord God had made. And he said to the woman, "Has God indeed said, 'You shall not eat of every tree in the garden'?"
>
> And the woman said to the serpent, "We may eat the fruit of the trees of the garden, but of the fruit of the tree which is in the midst of the garden, God said 'You shall not eat it, nor shall you touch it, lest you die.'"
>
> Then the serpent said to the woman, "You will not surely die. "For God knows that in the day you eat of it your eyes will be opened and you will be like God, knowing good and evil."
>
> So when the woman saw that the tree was good for food, that it was pleasant to the eyes, and a tree desirable to make one wise, she took of its fruit and ate. She also gave to her husband with her, and he ate. (Genesis 3:1–6)

The serpent in this dialogue is no other than the devil himself. Through these verses, we can see how Satan operates. He tries to tempt you to make the wrong choice. The temptation in this case involved fruit that looked pleasant to the eye and had the promise of newfound knowledge. You may ask, "What is the harm of eating a piece of fruit that has the benefit of giving you wisdom?" The harm is God warned Adam not to eat the fruit of the tree of the knowledge of good and evil, and God's caveats always keep us from harm.

Adam and Eve may not have understood the problems that would result from not listening to God, but they should have trusted His word to keep them out of trouble. Besides, God had already provided Adam and Eve with an abundance of provision, and there was no need to eat the forbidden fruit.

As for the increased knowledge, Adam and Eve's thought process before they ate the fruit was the same as God's. They were both created in the image of God, which meant they thought and acted perfectly like God does. Eating the forbidden fruit did not increase their knowledge but changed and corrupted their minds so they no longer reasoned the same as their Creator.

You may think, *I would have not been tempted to eat that fruit.* This may be true, but everyone has a weakness. What may be tempting to you may not necessarily tempt me. For some people, an alcoholic beverage may not interest them at all, and others can drink it in moderation without ill effects. For other people, however, an addiction to alcohol is a tool that Satan uses to destroy their lives. We all can be tempted, and the devil will search out your weaknesses until he eventually finds them. The Bible describes the devil as cunning, and he will not stop looking until he finds the hole in your shield. When Satan identifies your soft spot, he will do everything in his power to exploit that vulnerability.

How does the devil find and exploit your weakness? He will probe you by introducing doubt into your life to see if you will question the truth. Satan told Eve, "You will not surely die." Through this manipulation, the devil was trying to get Eve to question the authority of God and ask questions like, "Did I hear God right? Is He trying to withhold something from me by stopping me from eating the forbidden fruit?"

Satan tried this same strategy with Jesus in Matthew chapter 4 by beginning every temptation with the phrase, "If you are the Son of God." Satan was attempting to provoke Jesus to prove His identity by trying to get Him to display His power as evidence of His deity. Jesus did not question His identity or the authority of God but counteracted the statements with the truth, the Word of God. Jesus knew what His mission was, and He did not have to prove anything to anyone, especially to the devil. Jesus illustrated how we should fight temptation using the Word of God, for Satan has no defense against the truth.

If the truth was used in the conversation between Eve and the devil, the issue could have been quickly resolved by Eve simply responding with, "God told us not to eat the fruit of this tree." But instead of putting a stop to the temptation, Eve continued to listen to the lies of Satan as he persistently deceived her. This is what Satan does. He tells lies and bends the truth. God, on the other hand, is not capable of telling lies (Hebrews 6:18), and everything in His Word is designed for our good. The resulting death from eating the forbidden fruit involved a spiritual death as described in chapter 1. Adam and Eve could have avoided this spiritual demise by listening to God's counsel that was given for their benefit and not to restrict their freedom. We can either follow the commandments of God or listen to Satan, but be ready to pay the price if you chose to side with the devil.

Not listening to God got Adam and Eve into a lot of trouble, and the same can happen to you. You may ask, "Why did God put the tree of the knowledge of good and evil into the garden anyway? Was He not just setting Adam and Eve up for failure?" Far from the contrary, God gave us free will or the right to choose how we will conduct our lives. God will not force you to follow His command-ments or to love Him; the choice is yours to make. God supplied Adam and Eve with a beautiful garden filled with ample provision and gave man instructions not to eat from just one tree. It seems like a good deal when you look at it from this angle, but Adam and Eve chose the empty promise of the devil. Not listening to what God had told them was a costly mistake that lead to several problems.

One of the first matters noticed by Adam and Eve was their nakedness (Genesis 3:7). Why were they discerning this fact now? Were they not always naked? Their disobedience caused a shift in their perspective that resulted in their becoming aware of their nakedness. When they were serving God, the focus was on God and what God was doing in their lives. After the transgression, Adam and Eve began to focus on themselves, transitioning to self-centeredness instead of remaining God centered. When Adam and Eve's focus was on God, they did not notice their nakedness, but when they focused on themselves, their nakedness became apparent.

The perception shift can also be observed in the actions of Adam and Eve. Note that when Adam is questioned by God about the incident, the first thing Adam tries to do is blame God and Eve for his predicament. Adam tells God, "The woman who you gave to me, she gave me of the tree, and I ate" (Genesis 3:12). "It is your fault God for creating that woman! It's Eve's fault for giving me the fruit! It is not my fault!" Of course it was Adam's fault. God left him in charge of the garden with clear instructions not to eat the fruit produced by the tree of the knowledge of good and evil. What is even worse is in verse 3:6 of Genesis, it reveals that Eve gave her husband, who was with her, some of the fruit to eat. Adam was standing next to Eve the whole time during the temptation. It was his responsibility to stop the serpent in his tracks, but he stood idly by, choosing to do nothing while enjoying the forbidden fruit.

It also becomes evident the loving nature of God had died in Adam. He did not take responsibility for his actions but chose to blame everyone else who was involved. Satan is called the accuser of the brethren for his attacks against Christians. Observe how the actions of Adam after the Fall are now more closely in line with the characteristics of the devil. Eve displays a similar attitude when questioned by God as she shifted the blame for her disobedience onto the serpent. The wisdom they received from eating the forbidden fruit tainted the way they rationalized. The newfound knowledge was based on self-centeredness and not humility or love for others, thus counters the behavior of God.

Another change that transpired is when Adam and Eve hid from God. God, whom they had fellowshipped with before the Fall, now instilled fear in them. They had done something God specifically told them not to do, and this act of disobedience is called sin. The sin nature of Satan acquired through his disobedience against God was now being experienced by Adam and Eve through their own act of disobedience. The consequences of this sin separated them from God, who provided them with provision, companionship, happiness, and peace. The realization of these consequences by Adam and Eve probably filled them with dread and anxiety, while their sin-induced shame caused them to hide from God. To make matters worse, they were banished from the Garden of Eden. This is a pretty hefty price to pay for eating a piece of fruit, but sin will always cost you something.

By following the direction of the devil, Satan gained authority over Adam and Eve through sin and became their master. He had successfully separated them from God through his deception. In this life, you get to choose whom you will serve. If you listen to God and follow His commandments, you serve God. If you listen to the devil by not following God's commandments, you fall into Satan's trap, and you serve him. There is no neutral ground in the spiritual world. You are either for God or against Him.

The separation from God produced a lot of new experiences for Adam and Eve. In the garden with God, man was eternal and did not suffer death. After the Fall, man would not only be subjected to physical death of the body, but also spiritual death, which is eternal separation from God. When man was eternal, time did not exist. Time has no meaning in an eternal existence, but in our present lives, time is a dominant factor governing our daily schedules.

Also, the blessings of God were removed from Adam and Eve as sin ruled in their lives. Abundance turned to lack, peace turned to conflict, ease turned to toil, and pain was introduced to them. Most importantly, Adam and Eve became self-centered instead of remaining God centered. This self-centeredness or carnal nature has been passed down from Adam and Eve though the bloodline of mankind today. No one is born without being under the bondage of this sin nature, which leads to spiritual death.

From the above paragraphs, you can see how the injection of sin into this world has caused a whole lot of headaches. Sin took mankind out of paradise and substituted hardships and burdens in return. It seems Adam and Eve made one bad decision and now we must all pay the price. You may think it is unfair you have to experience hardship and suffering based on another person's decision, but sooner or later, each and every one of us would have succumbed to sin if placed in the same situation.

There is no need to worry, however, for God has a plan to conquer sin and return us to paradise. But before looking at this plan, let us first examine the impact of sin in the world and how it affects the way we live.

CHAPTER 3

The Time Trap

In the Garden of Eden, time was of no consequence before sin entered the world. The eternal life Adam and Eve lived was not constrained by time because eternity is an immeasurable quantity. After man had sinned, however, time became an integral part of our lives, leaving us a finite amount of time to spend here on earth. We must now adhere to a schedule that dictates how long we sleep, work, or go to school. We even have to account for our leisure time. The freedom once experienced in the garden does not exist in this life.

Time management has become an important facet in the modern world, and many people try to fill every second with activity. Phrases like "time is money" pushes people to better utilize their day. We have become so busy, there is barely a moment to think. Satan delights in this type of behavior because when we become so engrossed in our daily activities, our relationship with God will suffer. The longer the devil can keep us busy, the better the chance he has to completely separate us from knowing our Creator. Satan uses time as a powerful tool to impede our spiritual walk.

God is not subject to time because He is eternal. Measures of time such as past, present, and future do not apply to God. God is omnipresent, which means He exists everywhere at once, including the past, present, and future. However, the only time we can fellowship with God through prayer, worship, and studying His Word is in the present moment. Satan is aware of this and tries to pull us into the past or project us into the future, keeping our thoughts out of the present. There are many ways in which Satan is successful in operating in this manner.

The past can have a powerful attraction, anchoring people so they cannot move forward in their lives. Some people remember the good old days and are constantly reliving those past events. Others may recall past episodes, provoking thoughts of anger or shame. The past can also house thoughts of abuse or harm, generating emotions of fear. Living in the past can be a dangerous habit, so let's look at some of the consequences of this practice.

People who relive their glory days do so thinking the best has passed them by. Instead of looking at their current situation, they are always pining for the past. God wants you to have a better today, but you must be in the present moment for this to happen. If you are looking in the past, you are not paying attention to what God wants to do in your life now.

When the Israelites were slaves in Egypt, God wanted to free His people from their bondage under Pharaoh and bring them to the promise land. During the journey, the Israelites complained about the manna God had provided for them, and they began to reminisce about the fish, cucumbers, melons, onions, leeks, and garlic they had in Egypt (Numbers 11:5). The Israelites had totally forgotten about the brutal workload they were subjected to under the rule of the Egyptians. God had rescued them from captivity and provided for their needs, but they were blind to His kindness. The good old days were not that great for Israel, and God was trying to bring them to a better tomorrow.

God is continuously reaching out, trying to change us to become more like Him. In the process, He breaks the grip of Satan, and His blessings are released to us. We will not see God's blessings if our focus is always in the past. We must maintain our attention in the now, where we can react to the calling of God.

People who focus on their past mistakes experience a variety of different emotions. Sometimes anger is invoked due to this past event when a person realizes the stupidity of their actions. Other people may express guilt or shame in response to the acts they committed. In either case, people continue to beat themselves up for things they cannot change. The devil loves to use these past events to create bondages that anchor you in the past. God, however, wants to break these bondages and heal your pain. Guilt and shame are not emotions God wants you to carry around. When you turn these feelings over to God, you no longer have to be a slave to your past.

One of the most powerful tools the devil uses is unforgiveness for an infraction that happened in the past. The Bible teaches if we will not forgive the sins of others, God will not forgive our sins (Matthew 6:15). So if someone commits a wrongful act against you and you refuse to forgive them, you are cutting off your connection to God. Since unforgiveness separates you from God, which is your source of blessings, it benefits you to forgive others. These individuals who hurt you are probably not even thinking about you or the offense. The only person you are hurting is yourself, so do not let the devil win! Forgive, move on, and allow the blessings of God to flow in your life.

Just like we cannot change the past, we cannot control what is going to happen in the future. We cannot have total authority over the economy, the weather, or the way other people are going to act toward us. The only thing we can have total power over is the way we react to the circumstances that impact our lives. We can look for the bad in every situation and have a mindset of, "Why do bad things always happen to me?" This type of behavior sets us up for failure because whatever you concentrate on is going to expand in your life. If you focus on the bad news, it will fill your mind with despair and dread. The more you focus on what is going wrong in your life, the more these emotions intensify. But if you look on the bright side of the situation, you can usually find something good.

Joseph son of Jacob was sold into slavery, thrown into prison for an offense he did not commit, and was forgotten by the people he assisted to get released from prison. As bad as this portion of his life was, the experiences prepared Joseph so he would flourish and become the second most powerful man in the world (Genesis 37–50). In that capacity, he was not only able to save his starving family but also all of the known world. What the devil meant for evil, God used for good. Look for the silver lining in every trial and see how God will use your difficulties in ways you never thought were possible.

Some people will continually delay their joy and happiness to some future event. "When I win the lottery, then my life will be better. Once I find a new job more suited for me, I will finally be happy." The problem is while people are waiting for that future event to happen, they are usually miserable. The sad part is what they are hoping for may never happen.

If we would just look at our present situation and count our blessings, we could see how truly fortunate we are. There are a lot of people who have it a lot worse off than you. Concentrate on what is going good in your life instead of what is bad because if you are focusing on the problem, you cannot see the solution. Life is a process where we grow and learn. Finding a solution to your problem will allow you to change your life for the better and prepare you to solve future challenges. If you do not enjoy your present situation, there is no guarantee the future will be any better. Enjoy what you have today, and that joy will be carried over into your tomorrow.

Worry is probably the biggest time waster we have in our lives. As humans, we worry about the future of our finances, relationships, and many other perceived problems that usually never materialize. Worry is also a double-edged sword. You can also worry about things you did in the past. In both cases, there is no need to worry because worrying is not going to change anything. Worry consumes your present moment, which is better spent communing with God. Proverbs 3:5–6 suggests we "trust in the Lord with all your heart and lean not on your own understanding. Acknowledge Him and He will direct your path." You do not know what the future is going to bring, but God does. God wants the best for you, so why worry? Whether you are worrying about the past or the future, allow God to direct your path while you trust in Him.

Your time here on earth is valuable, and God put you in this world to accomplish something special. Everyone has a purpose that completes a piece of the puzzle. Our time is better utilized talking to God about our problems through prayer—yes, prayer! Prayer is the communication tool we use to tell God how we feel. In order for communication to work, however, it must be a two-way street. You can talk, but you also have to listen. God's answer can come by reading the Bible and meditating on His Word. Seeking God through quiet time or worship is always a good way to find wisdom.

If you truly seek God, you will find Him. Do not fall into the devil's trap and allow him to steal your God-given time. The devil wants to destroy you, but God will raise you up. Stay in the present moment and use your time wisely.

CHAPTER 4

Stressed Out

In Luke 10:38–42, a scene plays out where Jesus visits the home of Martha and Mary. Martha is busy taking care of the hospitality, while Mary is sitting at the feet of Jesus, listening to Him speak. Martha is a little perturbed by this situation and asked Jesus if Mary can help her with the preparations. This seems like a fair question, but Jesus answers with the following verses from Luke 10:41–42: "Martha, Martha, you are troubled about many things. But one thing is needed, and Mary has chosen the good part, which will not be taken away from her."

Some observations can be taken away from this scripture. First, Jesus was not condemning Martha's service but the manner in which she performed that duty. Jesus can see Martha is anxious. She may have been worrying about getting the preparations just perfect for the guest or contemplating how failing at this task would hurt her reputation. Whatever the case, Mary is in perfect peace at the feet of Jesus. She is at peace because the words of Jesus are truth, and truth chases away anxiety like light chases away darkness. Jesus was not going to let Martha pull Mary from a position of peace to a condition of worry or anxiety.

The world will always try to pull you out of a posture of peace. In this fast-paced world, people are pushing to get involved in more activities than ever. People are trying to raise a family while pursuing a career and keeping an active social life. All this striving to achieve this covenant lifestyle is driving stress levels up. People have more anxiety and worries today than probably any time in history. Stress-related illnesses are on the rise due to this accelerated climate. This stress-inducing lifestyle is causing people to miss out on the life God truly wants them to have, a life of peace. God's plan was for man to live and flourish while being in communion with Himself. Eden before the first transgression was a place free from worry and anxiety because it was filled with the presence of God. The peace Adam and Eve once had in the garden cannot be achieved by using the world's standards but can be obtained by saturating ourselves in a relationship with God. God is the only true path to peace and joy on this earth.

Where did this worry and anxiety originate from? The root of anxiety and worry is fear, and fear makes its first appearance after the Fall of man. God was visiting the garden in the cool of the day as was customary, but Adam and Eve did not come out to greet Him. When God called out to them, Adam answered and said, "I was afraid because I was naked and I hid myself" (Genesis 3:10). Why was Adam afraid? Was his sin made apparent in the presence of a holy God? Was he alarmed by the new knowledge obtained by his disobedience? We may never know why Adam was afraid, but this fear did accomplish one thing: it separated man from God. Fear is not a characteristic of the Lord God. The traits of God are love, joy, peace, patience, goodness, kindness, gentleness, faithfulness, and self-control (Galatians 5:22–23). There is no fear in the Spirit of God.

Let's take a closer look at fear. Amazingly enough, some fear may be beneficial. Fear of the Lord is a healthy sentiment based on honor and reverence for God. This type of respect for God should be present in everyone's life. In addition, fear that causes you to react to some immediate threat such as moving out of the way of an oncoming vehicle will probably save your life. This type of fear is short-term in duration and is followed by a response to action.

Fear that is long-term in nature and paralyzes you or results in no corrective action is destructive. We can use fear of flying as an example. Yes, planes do crash, and when they do, many people will usually die. But air travel is one of the safest modes of travel, and these incidences rarely ever happen. Airplanes can take you to places where other modes of travel cannot. So dying in an aircraft-related accident is possible but not very likely. In fact, like the fear of flying, most of the things we worry about do not even happen. Therefore, anxiety caused by worrying about flying could keep a person from exploring new cultures, visiting family who lives far away, or opening lucrative business opportunities in distant lands. Fear that generates worry, dread, or anxiety is a tool of Satan used to keep you from reaching your full potential. These are the type of fears we will explore.

So how do we combat fear? Before we can overcome fear, we have to know what it is. Let us see if we can describe fear. Can we see fear? No, fear does not have any visible qualities. Can we touch fear? No, fear is not tangible. As a matter of fact, fear cannot be quantified by our five senses of touch, sight, sound, taste, or smell. So what is it? The answer to this question is found 2 Timothy 1:7, where Saint Paul states, "God has not given us a spirit of fear, but of power, love and sound mind." If fear is a spirit that is not from God, then it can only come from a place of evil.

So how do we take a defensive position against the spirit of fear? Many battles involving fear begin in the mind. The devil will present a seed of anxiety or worry to you in an effort to get you to receive it. A seed can only grow when it is planted in good soil and it is nurtured. You receive the seed and plant it in good soil if it gets your attention. If you begin to continuously think about the issue, you are now nurturing the seed, and it will begin to grow. The more you worry about the issue, the more it will grow until it encompasses your whole thought process.

So how do we stop the seed from growing? We simply think of something else. Apostle Paul suggests we think about whatever is true, noble, right, pure, lovely, admirable, excellent, and praiseworthy (Philippians 4:8). When you think about how many good things you have going on in your life, it seems foolish to spend your time worrying about the bad. A sound mind should only dwell on good things and minimize the bad. God is good, and He wants to be an integral part of your life. He fulfills all the descriptors mentioned in the above scripture, making Him the perfect focal point. So it pays to continuously reflect on Him and His Word.

Further advice in Philippians 4:6 outlines that we should "be anxious for nothing, but in prayer and petition, with thanksgiving, make your request known to God." When we do this, the peace of God fills our hearts and our minds, allowing us to be in complete ease. It is impossible to fight the devil without God, Who has the power to break the bondages that will free you from the worries of this world. God promises to supply all our needs through the glorious riches in Christ Jesus (Philippians 4:19), so there is no need to stress. Be diligent and read the Word of God, putting all its wisdom into practice.

The love God has for us is unimaginable, and He wants to help us. He listens to our prayers and responds, but you must believe He will work things out for your good. In verse 6, it says to pray and petition while giving thanks. *Petition* means to plead or ask again and again. You may think, *Why do I have to pray over and over? Doesn't God already know what I need?* Yes, God knows what you need before you ask because He is all-knowing. The repetition is for your benefit, so you will focus on God and not on your problem. When your focus is totally on God and not on your anxiety, God can work miracles in your life. This does not mean your life will be problem-free, but you should experience some level of peace while going through the trials.

The last step, giving thanks, seals the deal. You only thank someone when they have done something or are about to do something for you. Giving thanks acknowledges your expectation that God is going to take care of you.

Love is also a powerful tool against fear. The Bible states, "There is no fear in love, but perfect love cast out all fear" (1 John 4:18). God's love for you is so complete, there is nothing you can do that will make Him not love you. He died on the cross for you. Anyone who is willing to die for you must have a considerable affection toward you. Like a parent who protects their children from harm, Father God wants to protect you from evil. With that kind of love, why would you fill your life with anxiety and worry? The more we love God and trust in Him, the less we will fear. Don't worry. God can handle all of your problems! Once you begin to understand how much God loves us, fear will not be able to flourish in you.

We have talked about love and a sound mind as defensive tools against fear and the enemy. There is also an offensive tool you can use against Satan, which is the power of God. This power and authority is given to all Christians who have a relationship with Jesus. Luke 10:19 states God has given us authority over all the power of the enemy, and nothing will harm us. When you think about it, you are only afraid of something when you believe it has the power to harm you. With God's protection, you are free of that fear.

It is important to remember this authority and power comes from God and not through any authority or power we possess. This power is accessed by trusting in God to help you. An example of this can be found in Daniel chapter 3, where Shadrach, Meshach, and Abednego refused to worship King Nebuchadnezzar's statue of gold. The king told the Hebrew boys if they did not worship the statue, they would be burned in the furnace. The three replied to the king, "We do not need to defend ourselves before you in this matter. If we are thrown into the blazing furnace, the God we serve is able to save us from it, and He will rescue us from your hand" (Daniel 3:16–17).

What a brazen response to the king. They knew worshipping an idol was wrong and would not betray their beliefs. So into the furnace the boys went. Instead of dying a horrible death, Jesus met them in the flames, and they came out of the furnace unharmed. They did not even smell of smoke, and even the bondages binding them were released. They took their God-given authority over evil and trusted God with their very lives.

Not only did God save them, He blessed them with a promotion in a land that was not their own. But before they received the blessing, they had to walk in the fire. Not many people like to go through pain and hardship. Most of us would have probably not gone into the furnace, but total trust in God allows you to have the confidence that He will take care of you in your trials.

If we confront fear with power, love, and a sound mind, we can overcome it. When bad things or situations come into our lives, your position of power is a state of peace. The world's behavior may be one of worry, but this is not what God intended for you. We are to imitate God, not the world.

As we take a look at Jesus in Luke 8:22–25, we find Him asleep in the stern of a boat in the midst of a powerful storm. As the boat begins taking on water, the apostles who accompanied Him became fearful for their lives, and in a panic, they awakened Jesus. Jesus did not share their concern but kept His peace while He addressed the storm, causing it to cease. You cannot chase away worry and anxiety when you are consumed in it. Address your problems from your power position, a posture of peace.

As we journey through life, we will always run into storms. Do not allow the storms to steal your peace. Remember, Jesus is in the boat with you, and He can calm any storm. Trust in Him and watch your fear melt away.

CHAPTER 5

Life Abundant

Have you ever thought about where your next breath was coming from? We breathe hundreds of times in a single day, but we never give it a second thought even though air is one of the most important elements we need to survive. You can live several weeks without eating. You can live a week without water, but if all the air was taken out of the atmosphere, within minutes, we would all cease to be alive. Yet we pollute our environment and the very precious air we need to live without considering the consequences.

How is it we can breathe freely and not even be concerned with where our next breath is coming from? That is because air is abundant. There is so much air in the atmosphere, we never have to give a thought about how to supply our needs. In a world saturated in commercialism, air is a free commodity. No one would ever think about paying for the air we breathe because there is so much of it. If gold was as abundant as air is, it would be worthless. Air is highly abundant, but it is our most valuable resource.

In John 10:10, it states that God wants us to live life abundantly. God is the One who engineered the world's ecosystem so we would have all of the air we need to survive and more. God not only wants to meet our needs but to exceed them. In the Garden of Eden, all of the provisional requirements of Adam and Eve were accommodated abundantly, and they did not have to worry about how their necessities were going to be supplied. Like the air we now breathe,

the first occupants of this world probably did not give this lifestyle a second thought. It was a life blessed beyond measure with provision provided in abundance by God.

If God is able to supply all of our needs in abundance, why is there so much lack in the world today? In Genesis 3:17, God tells Adam since he listened to his wife and ate the fruit of the tree he was instructed not to eat, "Cursed is the ground because of you: through painful toil you will eat of it all the days of your life." Being disobedient to what God had commanded Adam to do had a costly consequence. The abundance of God was traded for the lack of Satan. Living in a world under the influence of Satan creates a system of apparent lack with only a limited amount of resources to go around.

So is there truly lack in the world today, or is it our perception? The answer to both parts of this question is yes. If we look to the world to supply our sustenance, there is always going to be a lack mentality. You will never have enough money, resources, or ability to meet your needs. That is exactly what the devil wants you to believe. Satan does not want you to experience security but only hopelessness and dread. But if you look to God to supply your provision, then you can tap into life abundant. God will meet your needs and provide extra so you have the ability to bless others. The provision of God does not know any limits, and like the air we breathe, it comes in abundance.

This abundance is illustrated in John 6:1–14, when Jesus is feeding the five thousand. At the beginning of chapter 6, it describes a great multitude of people who have followed Jesus to a remote place. Jesus teaches the people, but as evening approaches, Jesus asked the apostles where they could buy food to feed the masses. The number of men present was approximately five thousand, but this did not include the members of the men's family who traveled with them.

Apostle Phillip responded to this request by saying eight months of wages could not provide enough food for every person to have a bite (John 6:7). The apostle was basically vocalizing his belief that this request was impossible. Everything seems impossible until someone accomplishes the impossible. People at the start of the 1900s would have never imagined air travel would be possible until the Wright brothers successfully took flight in 1903. Even with the advent of flight, the same people would have probably never guessed a trip to the moon was in the future. If man can perform these great feats, how much more can we accomplish with God? With God, nothing is impossible (Matthew 19:26).

In verse 6, the scripture describes a boy who has five barley loaves and two small fish. This is hardly enough to feed a multitude of people. The world would view this contribution as insignificant, but notice the posture of the child. He is sacrificing all he had to Jesus because he is not thinking of himself but of others. Jesus quickly commands the people to prepare to eat as He gives thanks for the food. The food was distributed to the people, and everyone ate as much as they wanted. After the meal was finished, there were still twelve baskets of food leftover. This is the power of the blessing of God, a blessing of abundance.

The boy is a representation of who we are in the kingdom of God. While the world may look at us as inconsequential with not much to offer, God sees us as abundant. He can take any talent or possession we have and bless it to build His kingdom. Most people align themselves with the beliefs of this world that state anything we possess is too small to make any large impact. This prevents them from offering themselves freely to God so they can be used by Him. If we could change our mindset to see ourselves as God sees us, this world would be a very different place.

So how do we beat the devil and tap into the abundance of God? In 2 Chronicles 1:7, God appears to Solomon and said to him, "Ask! What shall I give you?" Now Solomon could have asked for anything, but what he really wants is to honor the memory of his father and do well in his new position as king. In verse 10, Solomon asked God for wisdom and knowledge so that he can be a better ruler. Look at God's response:

> Because this was in your heart, and you
> have not asked for riches or wealth or honor or
> the life of your enemies, nor have you asked for
> long life-but have asked for wisdom and knowl-

edge for yourself, that you may judge My people over whom I have made you king-wisdom and knowledge are granted to you: And I will give you riches and wealth and honor, such as none of the kings have had who were before you, nor shall any after you have the like. (2 Chronicles 1:11–12)

Imagine if you could have all the wealth, respect, and happiness you could dream of with a healthy and long life. This is what Solomon received, but it was not what he asked for. He asked for the wisdom and knowledge of God so he could better serve His people. Solomon was not thinking of himself but how to serve others. Solomon's posture was not one of self-centeredness but one of selflessness. Because of this posture, God opened the windows of heaven to enrich the life of Solomon. By using this wisdom and knowledge he asked for, God allowed Solomon to be the richest king of all times.

The wisdom and knowledge of God are powerful tools in creating abundance. Let's face it. Who are the richest people in the world? People who have wisdom and knowledge can create wealth and keep it. Have you ever heard about people who have won large amounts of money in lotteries, only to lose it in a short amount of time? This was because they lacked these two traits.

And when your focus is on serving others, God will supernaturally bless you abundantly. Matthew 6:33 says, "Seek first the kingdom of God and His righteousness and all things will be provided to you." As you seek God first in all you do, He will provide for all your needs. This does not necessarily mean money but any resources needed to build His kingdom. This provision may not always come the way you expect it to, but God's ways are better than our own, so tap into the abundance of God by using the wisdom and knowledge outlined in God's Word.

Another factor needed to realize the abundance of God is illustrated in 1 Kings 17:8–16. These verses depict the events of Elijah the prophet and his introduction to a widow in Zarephath. Before this encounter, Elijah was being supernaturally sustained by ravens bringing him meat and bread, while he drank from a brook. After the brook dried up because of a great drought in the land, God then tells the prophet to visit the widow, who would now provide for him. This situation may be more ironic than the meat-eating ravens delivering his meals because widows of biblical days were usually some of the poorest people. Women of this time were not held in high regard and did not have a lot of career paths. Without the support of a man, this usually meant they were destined to have a meager existence.

The scene starts with Elijah's meeting the widow and asking for a drink of water. After this request, the prophet boldly asked for a piece of bread. Look at the response of the widow:

> As the Lord your God lives, I do not have bread, only a handful of flour in the bin, and a little oil in a jar; and see, I am gathering a couple of sticks that I may go in and prepare it for myself and my son, that we may eat it and die. (1 Kings 17:12)

Notice the desperation in her plea. This is a situation of great lack. Although the widow has some provision, it is not enough to keep her and her son alive. The condition of lack is always the same. What you have never seems to be enough to meet your needs, causing the situation to seem hopeless. In today's society, lack is a stark reality for many people.

Elijah is not taken back by this response. Instead, he then requests the widow make him a small cake and bring it to him. He promises that God will supply enough flour and oil to meet the needs of her household until the drought is over. The widow now has to make a choice: stick with the sure thing and keep her provisions or trust that the prophet is telling her the truth and make him some bread. If she sticks with the sure thing, the widow will have food but only enough to sustain her for a short while. If the prophet is telling the truth, she will not run out of flour and oil. For most of us, this would be a hard decision to make.

The widow does have one piece of knowledge. She knows that Elijah is a prophet, and this is evident in the beginning of verse 12, where she says, "As the Lord your God lives." By making this statement, she is confirming that Elijah is indeed a man of God and can be trusted. Secondly, by performing this selfless act, she is following God's second most important commandment of loving your neighbor (Matthew 22:39). Even though the widow believes Elijah is a prophet and knows she is doing God's will, it still takes a great deal of faith to give your child's bread away. Fortunately, the widow makes the right choice.

To taste the abundance of God, you must take risks, meaning you must have faith. The Bible states without faith it is impossible to please God (Hebrews 11:6). Having faith that God will come through for you is an essential part of receiving abundance. Like a child who trusts their parents to provide for them, we must have this same bond with God.

The next point on how to operate in abundance also involves a story about another widow and prophet. In 2 Kings 4:1–7, a widow had defaulted on a loan, and her creditor was coming to take her two sons as payment to make them slaves. As explained previously, a woman in biblical times was usually supported by a man, which could have been her father, husband, or son. In this case, not only would the widow lose the sons she loved, but she would probably lose her only means of financial support.

The widow then sees the prophet Elisha and explains her situation. Elisha asks the widow what she has of value. The widow explains she possesses only one jar of oil. Elisha then tells the widow to get as many empty containers as possible, instructing her to pour the oil from the jar she owns into the empty receptacles. The prophet assures her that after she completes this action, the containers she has collected will be filled with oil.

As in the scenario with the other widow, this act would take a lot of faith in addition to something more. It would take a level of expectation. If the widow did not believe the prophet, she would not have collected many jars, if any at all. If the widow's level of expectation was high and she believed the prophet, her abundance would be determined by the number of containers she collected. If you plant only a few seeds, you will not receive much of a harvest. A lot of times, we will pray for God's help but expect very little to happen. In order to taste the abundance of God, we must have big expectations because our God is a big God.

After the widow hears the word of the prophet, she collects as many containers as she could find. As she poured the oil into the jars, each one was filled. The final result was the widow had such abundance she paid off all her debt and had enough to live on. The amount of her abundance was proportional to her expectation. There are times when God will ask you to use what you have and trust in Him to bless it. The widow only had one jar of oil, but her faith and expectation allowed God to turn her lack into abundance. This can be hard to do, especially when you are experiencing lack. The decision to trust God and expect Him to help us is ours to decide.

So by using wisdom, knowledge, faith, and expectation, we become children of abundance. These factors by themselves will not guarantee us success. We must acknowledge that abundance is a direct result of God's blessing due to the relationship we have with Him. As we work with God to perform His will for our lives, He will direct our paths and supply us with what we need for the journey.

CHAPTER 6

The Struggle

*And I will put enmity between you and the woman,
and between your offspring and hers; he will crush
your head, and you will strike his heel.*

—Genesis 3:15

Jesus talked about the end of the age and some of the signs we should be looking out for. He described that nations would rise against nations, and there would be wars and rumors of wars. Jesus talked about betrayal, persecution, hatred, and that the love of many would grow cold (Matthew 24:6–12). This is a perfect outline of what is happening in our world today. Nations are fighting or threatening other nations in an attempt to jockey for a higher position in the world arena. There is social unrest with racial tensions running high. Crimes once considered to be unthinkable just years ago are now commonplace. Mass shootings in schools, parents killing their own children, spouses killing spouses, and other such debauchery dominate the news headlines on a daily basis. It would seem the hearts of many have grown cold in this generation.

Before the Fall, there was no conflict in the world. Everything was in perfect harmony under the direction of the Spirit of God. Once the sin nature entered into humanity, the harmony of God on earth was quickly eroded away. The first murder can be witnessed between two brothers, the offspring of Adam and Eve. Cain, who worked the soil, presented some of the fruits of his labor to God as an offering, while Abel presented portions from the firstborn of his flock. God found Abel's offering to be acceptable but rejected Cain's gift. God consulted with Cain to correct his behavior, but Cain did not heed His advice. Instead, Cain lured Abel out to the field then attacked and killed his brother in a jealous rage (Genesis 4:2–8). Since this first dispute, conflict has secured its place in our lives. The Bible verse "a little yeast works its way through the whole loaf" (Galatians 5:9) is a good description of how quickly sin can spread.

Satan would like nothing better than the world to be in total chaos. Wars kill thousands of people without Satan having to move a muscle. Crimes that involve killing others not only affect the person being murdered but will also corrupt the one who is performing the act. Having God's creation kill each other makes the devil's job easy, but this act is in direct violation of God's commandment, which condemns murder. God wanted us to love our fellow human beings and not inflict harm on them. As children of God, we should be united in fighting against the devil. He may strike at our heels, but through Jesus, we have the power to crush his head. This is impossible to do when God's creation is fighting each other.

What does the Bible say about how we are to deal with conflict? Matthew 5:39–41 outlines the position we should take when adversity comes into our lives. These verses state we should…

> Not resist an evil person, but whoever slaps you in your right cheek, turn the other to him also. If anyone wants to sue you and take away your tunic, let him have your cloak also. And whoever compels you to go one mile, go with him two.

This does not mean we should just allow people to take advantage or inflict harm upon us, but it means to not retaliate against the other person. When someone attacks you unprovoked, you have done nothing wrong. However, when you strike back at that person, your retaliation is not in alignment with God's commandment to love others. The attacking person has also dragged you down to their level. The more you feed the conflict, the more the disagreement will escalate. This is a destructive activity and one that is demonic in nature. God said to love your enemies and bless those who curse you (Matthew 5:44). If you act like your enemies behave, how are you any different than they are? By loving your enemies, you will be acting as God has intended you to act. The only possibility you have to change someone's heart is by loving them, not by acting with evil intent.

Acting as God has commanded us to act in a world where there is an eye-for-an-eye mentality is hard, but it will likely defuse a bad situation and neutralize it. Think of the many ways you can apply the wisdom of God to your daily lives. Your spouse is angry with you. You have two choices. The first choice is that you can defend yourself and fight back. This only makes the domestic dispute worse. Fighting against someone usually only makes them want to resist even more, but if you remain calm, your spouse will eventually stop yelling. For those who are married, this is a victory within itself. If you then pray for your spouse, God may work on their conscience so they realize their mistake and make amends. How many times could you use this template? How many times do you have problems at your job or school, with other family members, or even with complete strangers? Do not take revenge, but allow the Lord God to work it out for you. And for those situations that escalate out of control, always remember to be calm, for "vengeance is Mine, I will repay says the Lord" (Romans 12:19).

Conflict has permeated society, and you cannot live your life without running into an occasional crisis. There are several reasons why conflict could present itself. Conflict can come as a result of sin, which can generate an adverse reaction. For example, the decision Adam and Eve made to eat the forbidden fruit was in direct violation to what God instructed them to do. As you have realized by reading this book, putting their trust in the devil brought with it some very real consequences.

A lot of people believe you can sin and have no repercussions. Jesus is faithful and just to forgive your sin (1 John 1:9), but that does not mean you will be spared the punishment for your actions. A lot of the chaos we have in our lives is brought on by our own poor judgment. Bad decisions that lead to sin will always result in problems sooner or later. Avoid sin and reap the good things God intended you to have.

Crisis in your life can also be an attack of Satan. Most Christians who encounter trials believe they have done something wrong and are being punished. God is not vengefully waiting for you to make a mistake so He can punish you. You actually may be doing something that is in the will of God, and the devil is trying to break your focus. As recorded in Acts 16:16–34, Paul and Silas were visiting in Macedonia when they came across a slave girl possessed by an ungodly entity. Paul, under the influence of the Holy Spirit, cast the evil spirit out of the girl. The owners of the slave girl were angry with Paul and Silas because they used the girl's spirit of divination to make money. The two missionaries were then dragged off to jail and placed in stocks for performing a good deed. While in jail, the two did not despair but prayed and praised God. Suddenly, there was a great shaking, and the prison doors were flung open, while the prisoners' chains were broken off.

That is what God does! He open doors and breaks the bondages of Satan. It is hard to praise God in your trials, but always remember God is with you in your times of trouble. If we can keep our focus on God, He can take a bad situation and work it out for His glory. In the case of Paul and Silas, that is exactly what He did. The headmaster of the jail was awakened by the shaking and went to the prison to check on the inmates. When he saw all of the prison doors were open, he assumed the detainees had escaped. The jailer was about to commit suicide for this disgrace, but Paul stopped him before he could harm himself. Through a short conversation with the jailer, the man received salvation. Once again, God thwarted the devil's plan and made something good come from it! If Paul and Silas were more concerned about their present condition and did not praise God, they might have missed out on what God was trying to do. When trouble comes into your life, face it head-on with praise and prayers. God can take any crisis and turn it around for good.

God can also allow turmoil to come into your life for the purpose of testing and building your faith. God commanded Abraham to take his only son Isaac to Mount Moriah and sacrifice him. Although Abraham did not question God or complain about how unfair this task was, I am sure this request was a burden on his heart. The very next morning, Abraham began to travel to the destination of the sacrifice in compliance to God's wish. The journey to the mount was three days in duration, a long time for Abraham to think about what God had asked him to do. Imagine the anguish Abraham was experiencing knowing he would have to kill his child, but he did not waver in his obedience to God's request. He knew God would honor His covenant to build his legacy into a great nation, but an action of this magnitude takes a considerable amount of faith (Genesis 22).

As Abraham completes the journey, he takes his son up to the mountain and builds an altar. He then binds his son and places him on the stones to prepare him to be sacrificed. As Abraham raises the knife to plunge it into his son's chest, an angel of the Lord stops Abraham from committing this heinous act. If an all-knowing God knew Abraham would do what He asked him to do, what is the point of the exercise? God wanted Abraham to know there was nothing in his life, including his only son, that would come between him and God. This is an experience that surely stretched Abraham's faith and one which brought him closer to God. God is relational, and He wants nothing more than to strengthen the bonds of that relationship with you. God will use any situation in our lives to bring us closer to Him. That is how much He loves us.

As the world continues to march forward toward the end of the age, prompting the return of Jesus, the conflict between good and evil will increase. Those who serve God will experience more resistance from the devil as he attempts to derail God's plans. The world's culture will be in direct opposition with the faith as people pull away from God, seeking their own wisdom. Things will be turned upside down, and people will call evil things good and good things evil (Isaiah 5:20).

In the story about the wheat and the tares (Matthew 13:24–30), a farmer discovers tares among his wheat. When the farmer is questioned by his servants, he replies that the enemy must have sowed the bad seed in the field. He tells his servants to let the wheat and tares grow together and to separate them at harvest time. The farmer knows the wheat will grow and produce the fruit he desires in spite of the weeds, and then he will collect the grain and store it in his barn. The wise cultivator knows pulling up the tares will damage the crop and hinder the harvest, but letting the two grow together will strengthen the yield.

Just like the intelligent planter, God knows His people will produce godly results regardless of the evil and conflict that exist in the world. God's goodness shines brightest when seen in the backdrop of a dark world. His people are strengthened in adversity just as bricks are hardened in the furnace, and they will come out victorious despite the hardships Satan may put in their paths. Those who stand strong to the end of the age will reap their eternal reward when Jesus returns for His faithful ones.

God does not remove every crisis but allows us to flex our spiritual muscles so we can build endurance. It is faith in God that allows us to overcome the antics of the devil, causing us not to be weakened by chaos but prevail in the midst of it. We do not have to fear if we stand with God, for He will send Jesus to crush the head of the enemy. Conflict, chaos, and turmoil are here to stay, but we do not have to be overwhelmed by their carnage. Rely on Jesus to be your peace in times of crisis.

CHAPTER 7

Pushing through the Pain

And God will wipe away every tear from their eyes; there
shall be no more death, nor sorrow, nor crying. There shall
be no more pain, for the former things have passed away.
—Revelation 21:4

Imagine a place where there was no emotional or physical pain, a place where no tears were ever shed and every day was a joy, a place where sore joints and diseases do not exist. This is what life used to be like in Eden, but sadly, pain is a daily reality in most people's lives.

The first introduction of pain is realized in Eve's curse with the discomfort that is experienced in childbirth (Genesis 3:16). As any woman who has had a child can testify, the pain of childbearing is great, but after the suffering has diminished, the joy of a new life is celebrated. Pain is not eternal, and sooner or later, it will end. Like a pregnancy, the end of the pain will birth a new beginning.

Jesus said we would have trouble in this world (John 16:33). Jesus experienced His share of pain as He walked the earth performing the will of God. As Christians try to imitate the life of Jesus, we should expect to run into difficulties. Satan is going to try to throw you off balance by inflicting pain into your life, and he has a whole array of tools in his arsenal. It may be a bad doctor's report, death of a loved one, or a chronic illness.

Most of us will try to avoid pain if at all possible, but pain does have a useful purpose. Pain can tell us when we are touching a hot pan, and it is an excellent reminder of avoiding future discomfort. It can also be a warning sign that something is wrong with our bodies. A doctor can use the location of the pain and the description of the soreness to diagnose the sickness. A person who does not feel pain would be unaware they were touching something hot or were experiencing an illness. This situation could cause a more severe injury or would allow a disease to go untreated. Pain informs us there is something wrong when our body is experiencing some form of trauma.

What works in the natural world can also work in the spiritual. God can use pain to convey correction or expose us to some new revelation. Now God is not in the business of harming his creation, but in some situations, God will allow pain to expose an area of our life that needs to be changed. In Romans 5:3–4, it states we should rejoice in our sufferings because suffering produces perseverance, which produces character that eventually leads to hope. Now we do not rejoice for the pain we are feeling but in the knowledge our perseverance is being stretched.

We can compare it to working out in a gym. Muscle tissue will only strengthen and grow when you exercise with repetitions under resistance. The devil supplies the resistance; our repeated ability to overcome the pain increases our perseverance, thus changing our character. With this character change, we grow closer to God as we learn to trust Him, which gives us hope. Hope in Christ is the strength we need to overcome the issues of this world.

Apostle Paul received his fair share of suffering, and God used this pain to shape him into the man He wanted him to be. Paul received the very best training and sincerely wanted to serve the Lord God, but his initial viewpoint was a little distorted. The Pharisee of Pharisees was fighting the very God he had vowed to serve. Paul was on a mission to persecute God's people when Jesus met him in a flash of light on the road to Damascus (Acts 9). This meeting blinded Paul for three days until a man named Ananias prayed for his sight, an action also resulting with an infilling of the Holy Spirit. After this event, Paul started on a new adventure preaching the revelation about Jesus that was deposited in him. His eyes were opened to the truth in spite of the discomfort he suffered.

Even as a changed man under the guidance of God, Paul still experienced bouts with pain. In 2 Corinthians 12:7–9, Paul describes a thorn in his flesh given to him by Satan but used by God to keep him humble. The thorn (whether physical or emotional) must have caused great discomfort because Paul pleaded with God three times to take his suffering away. God's reply to Paul was, "My grace is sufficient for you, for My power is made perfect in weakness" (verse 9). God did not want Paul to become puffed up again and return to his old religious ways but for him to remain weakened by the thorn so God could work mightily in his life. Remember, God does not need our help but wants to work with us and through us to change the world. Therefore, God used the pain inflicted by Satan as a reminder not to veer off of the path the Holy Spirit was directing him to travel.

Paul's journey with God was not one absence of trials. He was beaten with rods three times, received forty lashes, shipwrecked three times, spent time in prison, and was in danger from his own countrymen. Paul persevered above all of the tribulations and overcame every persecution (2 Corinthians 11:23–27). Throughout the trials, Paul's love for God never wavered, and he served Him with all his heart. It is during this suffering God inspired Paul to write a large majority of the New Testament while he was in prison. Paul was truly changed for the better even though he went through some very trying times. So we can see by this example even those who serve God wholeheartedly are not exempt from difficulties.

Very few people have experienced the level of pain Job felt. First, there was the emotional pain of losing his family and all his worldly possessions. Then there was the physical pain of being subject to boils covering his whole body. Not even Job's wife had any sympathy for him. That's tough! Now God did not personally cause the pain Job suffered, but He allowed the devil to have free access to harm Job as long as he promised not to kill him.

You may think it was unfair to Job for God to pull back His protection and allow the devil to have his way, but God is always in the process of changing us. God wants you to understand how much

He loves you and how much He desires to have a relationship with you. Sometimes He uses drastic measures no matter how unfair it seems to us because God knows the best way to get our attention.

Jesus talks about the process of change being compared to the pruning of a vine. Jesus said, "Every branch in Me that does not bear fruit He takes away; and every branch that bears fruit He prunes, that it may bear more fruit" (John 15:2). When God cuts away the dead things in our lives, we may perceive the pruning as pain or loss, but the final result is a godlier you. As pruning a tree allows the nutrients to produce more fruit instead of supporting unproductive branches, God's pruning of your life removes the sinful, useless elements so the goodness of God can grow in you.

As Job began to contemplate the reason for his dilemma, Job's friends told him his problems were probably caused by some sin in his life, but Job proclaimed his innocence. As Job then began to complain and question God about his predicament, God then addressed Job in the form of a whirlwind. God spoke of His mightiness and questioned who Job was as compared to Him. God wanted to change Job's attitude, humble him, and bring him to the end of his self. God is sovereign, and His ways are not our ways (Isaiah 55:8), and it is sometimes hard to understand God's pruning process. Rest assured God wants what is best for us, and we have to trust Him in our pain. With this newfound perspective, Job prayed for his friends, focusing on them and not on his own problems, a practice that released God's double blessing.

Without the tribulation Job went through, he probably would have not been able to receive the revelation God was trying to communicate to him. Tough times and tragedy can do one of two things: drive us closer to God or further away. Many people would like to receive a blessing, but very few want to experience the suffering needed to get it. When people are suffering, they are often looking for the quickest way to resolve the pain without considering what God may be trying to do in them. Others blame God for their pain and distance themselves further from their only hope of salvation. Only those who focus on God instead of the pain have a chance of seeing His blessing.

In the story of Elisha and the Shunammite women (2 Kings 4:8–37), the Bible tells of such a blessing. When the prophet Elisha was passing through Shunem, there was a woman living in the area who supplied hospitality to him. To show his gratitude, the prophet inquired if he could do anything for her, but the woman was reluctant to request any favor. When Elisha discovers the woman was barren and that her husband was old, he prophesied to the woman, predicting she would become pregnant and have a child within a year. The woman can hardly believe her ears, but within the prescribed period of time, a son was born to her. Imagine the joy she experienced that day after being barren for so long.

The devil hates to see you happy and will do anything to try to steal your joy. With the Shunammite woman, the attempt to quench her happiness was through the death of her son. The emotional agony this woman felt must have been indescribable. First, she thought it was impossible for her to have a child; now he was being snatched from her. Instead of doing nothing, the woman is called to action and prepares to seek out the help of Elisha. When questioned by her husband why she is visiting the prophet, she replies, "It is well," without mentioning the death of the son. The woman then repeats the same phrase when greeted by Elisha's servant Gehazi. It is only when the woman embraces Elisha that the prophet senses her distress and accompanies the woman to her residence. Finding the child unresponsive, Elisha then prayed to God and ministered to the child until he was revived. The woman was then united back with her child, and the devil's attempt to break this women's spirit was overturned.

The emotional pain the Shunammite woman felt was indeed intense, but she did not allow the pain to deter her faith. By stating, "It is well," in response to this desperate situation, the woman steadied her focus on God instead of the pain. She firmly put her faith into action and sought out the one person who was able to help her. Elisha, filled with compassion for the woman's predicament, revived the dead child through the power of the Holy Spirit. The pain of this situation was great, but the goodness of God is greater.

Satan especially likes to dispense pain on believers who are serving God. Again, the devil wants people to focus on their pain instead of what God has planned for them. To illustrate this concept, I will use the actions of the apostles after the crucifixion of Jesus. The apostles were out in the temple area, preaching in the name of Jesus when they were arrested and brought to the religious council. Religious leaders were upset with the apostles for preaching about Jesus. They wanted His memory to fade away so they could reinstate their dominance over the people of Israel. The apostles were then threatened by the religious leaders and told to discontinue this practice, but they refused to listen. For this, they were beaten and given another stern warning not to mention the name of Jesus (Acts 5: 25–40). The desire of the apostles to please God outweighed any suffering they would experience. The Bible states the apostles rejoiced for the beating because they considered it to be a privilege to suffer for the name of Jesus (verse 41). In obedience to God's calling on their lives, they continued to preach about Jesus until their deaths.

I don't know about you, but when I face pain or suffering, the last thing I want to do is rejoice. But pushing through the pain is the only way to get to the other side and experience the blessings of God. The greater the pain, the greater the distraction, the bigger the blessing the devil may be trying to keep you from.

The utmost amount of pain anyone could have suffered was experienced by Jesus during His trial and crucifixion. Before He went to the cross, Jesus was severely beaten, whipped, mocked, and spit on. Then Jesus's hands and feet were nailed to a cross, where He would suffer a horrible death. If that was not enough, He was then separated from God the Father while He took on the sins of the world. No one has suffered as much as our Savior has. If the physical and emotional pain of Jesus's death was not enough, imagine the suffering of being exposed to every sin ever committed, a holy God exposed to an unholy culture, but Jesus pushed through the pain because of His love for you. Due to this effort, the greatest blessing the world has ever known was released as a free gift to all who would receive it. The devil could never inflict enough pain to stop Jesus from sacrificing His life to save you. That is how vast His love is for humanity.

Suffering is never pleasant, but you must remember, God is with you in your pain. Do not dwell on thoughts of why this trial is happening to you but instead focus on the might of God and seek His guidance in your situation. God will not waste any experience in your life in order to change you and bring you into a closer relationship with Him. A wonderful blessing may be waiting on the other side of that trial, so as bad as your pain is, always try to stay focused on God.

CHAPTER 8

It's All about Me

In the world today, everything is based on how quickly we can get our desires satisfied. We have fast food restaurants and microwave dinners, supplying us a variety of different entrées to appease any palate in a matter of a couple of minutes. Television offers programs on demand that supply an endless array of different entertainment venues. Modern cell phones provide us music to listen to, Internet access to social media or shopping, camera capabilities that take pictures and video, and many other features. What a big change from the past when home-cooked meals took time to prepare, television had only three stations, and a phone was just used to make calls.

It seems in order for a service or product to be successful in the marketplace today, the provider must find innovative ways to gratify our demands quickly in order to cater to our exact whim. This trend is getting more and more prominent in this current age. We impatiently wait for the next release of a cell phone or some new technology that promises to be the next greatest invention we simply cannot live without. We have become so engaged with our technology, we barely have time to do much else. People will spend multiple hours watching television or perusing social media, activities that feed our self-indulgence and increase the focus on pleasing ourselves.

The root of Adam is alive and well in today's society. In the first act of disobedience, Adam and Eve's self-centered pursuit of wisdom opened the door to the sin nature, which is now born into each and every one of us. This self-centered nature entices people to focus entirely on their own desires with little regard to the needs of others around them. In order to feed our self-centeredness, we claw our way higher on the economic ladder so we can fill our lives with more material possessions. But how much is enough? It seems no matter how much we obtain, we are always in pursuit of more, but we never are completely satisfied. Some of the wealthiest people in the world are still unhappy in spite of their money and possessions. How do we stop the madness?

Though gratifying our needs seems to be the path to fulfillment, this is rarely what is at the end of the journey. Why is this? The reason is you were made in the image of God, and His nature is to serve others, not to be self-serving. Our God nature is our true persona, and it is in constant battle with our self-centeredness. Serving others was the behavior Jesus displayed while He was on the earth. He came to do the will of the Father, who sent Him, which included healing the sick, casting out demons, raising the dead, and preaching the Word of God. Jesus did not come to be served but to serve others (Mathew 20:28). If the King of kings came to serve, how much more important is it for us to be servants?

We must fight the influence self-centeredness has over our lives and allow our hearts to be open to the Spirit of God. The only true way to experience joy is to walk out your God nature by imitating the life of Jesus. Most people would think it absurd to give their time, money, and resources to help other people they may not even know. The thought seems so ludicrous many do not even attempt to live the lifestyle of Jesus. But not living as God intended you to live is a big mistake because who knows you better than the One who created you? God commanded us to love Him first then to love our neighbor (Matthew 22:37–39) because this is what we were born to do. Serving God is displayed by loving and caring for His people. God wants the best for us, and His commandments are the way to wholeness and joy, which are achieved by adhering to the call of our God nature.

Love, unlike worldly measures, only grows when it is given away. The more you love, the more love is multiplied and in turn, the more love you receive. Love that is not given away diminishes and eventually dies. Whether people realize it or not, what they really desire is to be loved. When people do not feel like they are being loved, they unconsciously seek to fill the void through things like possessions, food, drugs, and alcohol in an attempt to feel good. These things make you happy for a little while but fail to keep you continuously satisfied because they cannot love you. Addictions are then formed in an attempt to sustain the short-term contentment, which causes further damage and positions the person further from the love they truly desire. Only God and people can love. This is why it is important to fellowship with others and worship the Lord your God.

Loving others can only be done if you are willing to be vulnerable. Most people do not want to open up their hearts, fearing they may be hurt. Love comes with a risk, and sometimes, there is pain involved, but love always prevails. The greatest example of love is when Jesus sacrificed Himself for you. When Jesus went to the cross, He was not self-centered in His actions but was more concerned with the fate of humanity. Jesus made Himself vulnerable and opened His heart for His creation, experiencing much pain in the process. Though Jesus's suffering was great, greater was His joy of setting you free. Through the love of Jesus, sin and the grave were conquered. Again, love always prevails!

So how do we go about loving and serving others? Some of the activities we should be doing are outlined in Matthew 25:35–36. It clearly illustrates we should be feeding the hungry, providing clothing for the needy, showing hospitality to strangers, and ministering to the sick and people in prison. This is the same kind of compassion Jesus displayed during His earthly ministry as He used His life to illustrate how we are to treat other people. Those who love Jesus and acknowledge this model during their lifetime will be rewarded by God with eternal life (verse 34). Those who reject this philosophy and only live to serve themselves will receive the due penalty for their lifestyle choice (verse 41). This does not mean we inherit eternal life through good works but perform these activities because of our love for God.

Serving was not meant to be a chore but should be a joyful extension of who you are. God has given each and every one of us a special talent or gifting. This talent usually comes so easily for the person to perform, they think anyone can do it. It may even be something really simple like being a good and thoughtful listener. Most people do not have the patience to listen to someone's problems with compassion and understanding. For the person who needs an ear to bend, your gifting may be the medicine they require.

Never underestimate the abilities God has given to you. As with the boy who gave his lunch to Jesus (feeding the five thousand), God can do mighty things through your gifting. Actions performed with love and kindness are the substance of things that can change the world. So whatever your gifting may be, use it to glorify God. Whether it is a smile, baking a cake for someone, or just being there for moral support, perform your gifting as onto the Lord! Joy will be released when you are actively using your abilities to bless others and to glorify God.

Whom do we serve, and who is our neighbor? This is the exact question a teacher of the law asked Jesus (Luke 10:25–37). This, in itself, was surprising because a teacher of his experience and expertise should have understood this concept, but he was blind to it. So Jesus tells the story of a Jewish man who was traveling when he was beaten and robbed. A priest came upon the man lying on the road, but not wanting to be bothered, he passed by without helping. Next approached a Levite, who also passed by the injured man without giving him any assistance. Lastly, a Samaritan came upon the wounded person. Unlike the priest and the Levite, the Samaritan bandaged the hurt man, put him on his own donkey, and brought him to lodging, where he paid for his expenses while the injured man healed. The irony of this situation is that the Samaritans were despised and looked down upon by the Jews, but the Samaritan was the only one who showed any compassion for the traveler. The priest and the Levite, Jews whose lives were set aside to serve God, reserved no pity for their fellow countryman. Only the Samaritan thought enough of the victim to help in his time of need.

The expert of the law is not much different than people today. A lot of people do not fully understand the concept of how they should be serving others. People pretend to be good like the priest and the Levite, but when it comes to applying the principles of God, most fall short of the mark. This is because most people do not have a trait the Samaritan possessed: humility. In Luke 18:9–14, the Bible talks about a Pharisee and a tax collector who went to the temple to pray. The Pharisee talked about how self-righteous he was and how he followed the letter of the law. The tax collector, however, confessed to God that he was a sinner in need of His mercy. The scripture states the tax collector was justified rather than the Pharisee.

Here, another ironic situation poses itself because the Pharisees were highly esteemed and considered pious, while the tax collectors were hated. Like the tax collector, the Samaritan was justified in God's eyes rather than the priest or Levite due to his humility. Self-righteousness and pride are the enemies of humility and usually prevent people from acting in God's will. We must think more of other people and less of ourselves if we are to overcome our self-centeredness and properly follow God's commandments. Life is not quantified by titles or position but by how we use our abilities to build the kingdom of God by loving others. The love of God can only flow through you when you possess true humility and are not consumed with self-centeredness. We must not do things out of selfish ambition but think of others as better than ourselves (Philippians 2:3).

It is easier to love people who treat you well, but it is much harder to love people who dislike you. The Bible states if you only love people who love you, how are you any different than worldly people (Matthew 5:46–47). As Christians, we are to be the light of the world, a peculiar people who stand out from the crowd. This means we should love our enemies and bless those who curse us (verse 44). Love is how we change the world. When you love people even when they treat you badly, sooner or later, they may begin to wonder why you are acting in this manner. This may open up the opportunity for you to share the gospel with them and free them from the clutches of Satan. Your actions will speak louder than any church sermon that can ever be preached. Loving your enemies puts your humility to the test, but just as Jesus did not complain or raise a hand to His accusers, so we are to be like Him. Do not allow pride to be a stumbling block in your service to God.

Today's society embraces the belief we can do whatever we want to. The adage "if you work hard, you can achieve anything you desire" is the modern banner for success. The only problem with operating in our own strength is that the devil is stronger and smarter than we are. Remember, the devil is your enemy, and he does not want you to be successful. He may allow you to achieve a certain measure of success as long as it dilutes the revelation of who God is, but his ultimate goal is to destroy you. Thinking that you are stronger or can outsmart the devil will only lead to your demise.

The only way to beat the devil is not to play his game. Do not be prideful and work in your own strength but humble yourself and allow the Lord God to lift you to victory. Pride makes a person believe they can make it on their own without God. Humility makes a person see their weaknesses and confesses their need for help from the Lord. All you have achieved in this world would not be possible if God did not give you your very next breath. Your strength, your very life, is sustained by God. Without Him, you would not be able to accomplish anything.

Samson is a perfect example of how a person can believe they are operating in their own strength, using the blessings of God to satisfy their own desires. Samson was born to be a Nazirite, which was one who was dedicated to God's service. There were certain rules that had to be followed when someone was consecrated to be a Nazirite. Candidates were not to drink fermented beverages, had to refrain from cutting their hair, and were not allowed to touch a dead body. Samson once killed a lion and then on a return visit, discovered a beehive in the carcass. Samson scooped out some of the honey and ate it (Judges 14:9). By touching the carcass of the lion, Samson made himself ceremonially unclean according to the Jewish customs and thus broke the vow of being a Nazirite. Samson was more concerned with appeasing his carnal nature than living true to a holy God.

Samson was dedicated to live his life for God, but he was mostly living his life for himself. He used his great strength to take revenge on his enemies. He had an eye for the ladies and often satisfied his desire for the opposite sex. Even with these flaws, God still used Samson to help rescue Israel from the control of the Philistines, an enemy of the state. Samson once killed one thousand Philistines with the jawbone of a donkey, an event of supernatural proportions. Did Samson praise God for delivering him from his adversaries? No, he arrogantly asked God if He was going to let him die of thirst or provide water for him to drink. This shows how self-absorbed Samson was and how he disrespected his anointing, using it only to gratify his carnal nature.

Most picture Samson to be a man who possessed a muscular body matching his great strength. I do not think that was the case. In Judges 16:5, it states the Philistines came to Samson's mistress, Delilah, and bribed her to find out what the secret was to his great strength. If his physique matched his strength, the answer to this question would have been obvious. That is why Delilah needed to search out the reason for his abilities. Delilah attempted to trick Samson three times in an attempt to discover the source of his strength without success. On the fourth try, Samson caved and released the reason for his great strength: the fact that his hair had never been cut. The real reason for his strength, however, was the power of God that surged in him when he faced times of trouble.

If Samson had given credit to God and said, "The Lord God gives me my great strength," no one would have been able to challenge him. Giving credit for his strength to his hair was a pathway to defeat. Besides, Samson defiled himself by touching the lion's carcass, and his strength did not diminish. It was not the violation of the law that caused the Spirit of God to leave but the absence of not giving the glory to God. With her newfound knowledge, Delilah quickly cut Samson's hair, and the Holy Spirit departed from him without his realizing it. Without the power of God, Samson was quickly overcome by the Philistine guards and was subdued. In this instance, Samson sold out his anointing in an attempt to appease his desires.

While in captivity, Samson was brought forth to perform for the Philistine nobles (Judges 16:23–30). Some three thousand men and women were present in a pagan temple area to witness the performance, where Samson was positioned between the main supporting columns of the structure. It is here Samson acknowledges the source of his true strength as he petitions God for one more burst of supernatural strength. Samson pushed against the pillars, and the temple fell, killing all who were inside.

God used Samson in spite of his faults, and God can work through you. Like Samson, we must give credit to God as being our true source of all good things. Just as Samson could have not moved those supports using his own strength, we cannot be successful without using the power of God that resides in us. In order for this to happen, we must empty ourselves of our carnal nature and allow God to rule and reign in our lives.

Taming self-centeredness is a task many people will not be able to accomplish. The seed of Adam planted into humanity at the beginning of civilization is in conflict with our God nature, a major disruption preventing many from fully reaching their spiritual apex. The only way to defeat this culprit is with the help of the Lord Jesus Christ. Accepting His free gift and building our relationship with Him are the only cure for the curse of self. So do not allow the characteristics of this world to shape your life, but be formed by your true nature, the Spirit of Christ.

CHAPTER 9

Battle Gear

All of the preceding chapters have described the changes that have taken place after the Fall of mankind. Adam and Eve came from a place of peace and entered into a world of moral decay that has evolved into chaos. We have studied some of the tools Satan uses to disrupt your life with the plan to ultimately destroy you, but you need not fear the devil if you are saved by God's grace. In His loving kindness, He has provided us with tools and protection against demonic forces.

This chapter will focus on the implements the army of God can utilize in this spiritual combat. While fighting this war, we must remember two things. First, the only way to win this battle is by putting control in God's hands, for God is our refuge and strength in our time of need (Psalm 46:1). There will be no victory in your life without God's help. Secondly, we do not fight against flesh and blood but against the spiritual host of wickedness (Ephesians 6:12). Our aim is to love people but to hate sin. People who are oppressed or possessed by demonic forces can be released from this bondage. Remember, we are all God's children, and we should treat others with the same grace Jesus has given us.

Before a soldier goes onto the battlefield, they must don the appropriate equipment. It is no different in spiritual warfare against the demonic elements of this world. No soldier would think of entering the battle without a weapon and the proper tools, but most

Christians enter this spiritual fight unprotected. The Bible clearly outlines the defensive and offensive measures we must take in order to defend ourselves. This armor includes the belt of truth, breastplate of righteousness, feet of readiness that comes from the gospel of peace, shield of faith, helmet of salvation, and the sword of the Spirit (Ephesians 6:13–17).

The first piece of protective equipment is the belt of truth. The definition of *truth* today has been severely skewed. The spirit of relativity has consumed this culture with every person having their own idea of what truth is. Satan loves this type of climate because the lines of truth become fuzzy and undefined. This behavior can be witnessed in Jesus's day when Pilate asked Jesus, "What is truth?" (John 18:38). Without any clear guidelines to what truth is, confusion can reign supreme as the devil uses this chaos to create deception. Fortunately, the Bible supplies us with God's truth, which is universal and absolute. In order to girdle your waist in truth, you first must know what truth is, which involves meditating on God's Word and adopting His truth as your own. Satan's lies have no power against the truth of God because lies cannot stand in the presence of truth.

After the belt of truth, you must wear the breastplate of righteousness. The breastplate is an important piece of equipment because it protects a vital area of the body, the heart. Police recognize the important of wearing a bulletproof vest to help protect them from the enemy. In a spiritual battle, the threat is not a bullet but the attacks from the demonic that attempt to quench the love in our hearts. This attack can only be stopped by righteousness, and since our righteousness is as dirty rags (Isaiah 64:6), we are unable to stop the devil in his tracks.

Jesus is the only person Who truly lived a righteous and perfect life, making Him impervious to the deception of Satan. Giving your heart to Jesus and trading your righteousness for His is the only way to protect it from the enemy. After receiving the righteousness of Jesus, confession and repentance of your sin maintains your righteousness, a practice that activates the power of the breastplate through the blood of Christ. Without repentance, you are fighting the devil on his level, a platform securing your defeat. Repent daily for your sins and allow the Lord Jesus Christ to cover you with His breastplate of righteousness.

How a person walks out their day-to-day journey can tell you a lot about their character. People whose life reflects the world's culture produce fruit in agreement with self-centeredness. This type of lifestyle is one the devil wants you to live, and it takes very little assistance from him to keep you on this path. Those who walk out their existence according to the gospel walk as Jesus did on this earth. They stand separate from the world and its beliefs, shining like the stars in the night sky. Walking in the knowledge and peace of the good news is powerful and attracts the attention of nonbelievers, which may lead them to inquire about your faith. Telling others about the scriptures and what Jesus did for us is like releasing information that can free prisoners of war from the devil's camp. You strike a blow against Satan by knowing the Bible and sharing it with others while also using it to repel his lies with God's truth. Feet of believers should always be ready to move and glorify God by spreading the good news of Jesus. This action propels the kingdom of God forward, snatching souls from the bowels of hell. So be prepared and have the feet of readiness that come from the gospel of peace as a part of your daily ensemble.

The shield of faith is a powerful defensive tool, which the Bible states can quench the fiery darts of the devil (verse 16). With faith or total trust in God and His Word, you can overcome anything Satan can throw at you. Faith allows you to accomplish impossible feats through the power of the Holy Spirit. You must remember, it is not enough just to possess the shield, but you must be able to hold it up in order to protect yourself. Not developing your faith is like having a shield down by your side, a position that offers very little protection and leaves you open to attack. If you develop your faith and hold your shield high, God will protect you against the evil one. Faith is so important that it will be expanded upon in a future chapter.

The helmet of salvation also protects a vital area, the mind. As mentioned in chapter 4, the mind is an internal battlefield where Satan will try to attack. A head wound can be a fatal injury, and care must be taken to guard against this harm. If he is allowed, the devil will plant doubt, fear, ungodly beliefs, and lies in your head, tempting you to dwell upon them. If Satan can get you to direct your focus on these falsehoods, the seed will grow and eventually consume you. You must know who you are in Christ, your only hope to stand; otherwise, you will be defeated. If you doubt your salvation and your relationship with God, you have given the devil a foothold to cause havoc. Communicate with God through prayer and by meditating on His Word, then the entranceways of your mind will be closed off from attack. Renew your mind in the ways of the Father and never forget to wear the helmet of salvation.

A sword is a tool that can be used as a defensive or offensive weapon. As a defensive instrument, the sword can be used to block the blows of an opponent. When fighting the devil and his demons, the sword of the Spirit, which is God's Word, can be used to block demonic lies. The more you know about the Bible and the more you apply it in your life, the better able you are to defend yourself. Having knowledge of God's ways is also like sharpening a sword, making it a more effective offensive weapon. The more heart knowledge about God you possess and practice, the sharper your sword becomes. The scriptures state, "the word of God is living and powerful, and sharper than any two-edged sword" (Hebrews 4:12). This weapon can pierce the thickest armor of your enemy. Again, when God is with you, the devil cannot stand against you. Wield your sword of the Spirit and conquer all the strongholds of the enemy.

It is always important to be prepared for an attack from the enemy. When a soldier is in a battle, they never let down their guard or take off their battle gear. The same principles apply to us when fighting this spiritual war. You must always have your armor on and must discern the possibility of an ambush. Sadly, most Christians do not consider the ramifications of walking out into the world without being protected. The world is our present battlefield, and trouble could be waiting for us right around the corner. This is why it is necessary to wear our armor and be ready to react to any adversity. The enemy is certainly ready to trip you up, so be prepared to rebuff any attack.

Not only is it important for you to wear the armor of God, but every good soldier always ensures their equipment is in good working order. There is no worse time to have a problem than when you are in the heat of the battle. Spiritual armor becomes stronger as your relationship with God grows. Make it a regular vigil to spend time with the Father, not out of obligation but out of love. Relationships are not cultivated without spending time with the other person. The same applies with God, so set time aside to spend with Him in prayer and reading His Word. As you do this, your armor will be better able to protect you. The more you grow in Christ, the better your protection will be.

Let's see how Jesus used this spiritual armor when He was here on earth. Jesus said, "I am the way and the truth and the life" (John 14:6). Jesus was truth, and He knew the Word of God because He was the Word (John 1:1). There are no gray areas in Jesus's belief system. The Father's truth was the truth, cut and dry. The devil can never defeat Jesus because He can void any lie through the power of God's Word.

The greatest commandment is to love the Lord your God with all your heart, mind, strength, and soul (Matthew 22:37). Jesus, who was without sin, followed the letter of God's law. His heart belonged to the Father wholly. The breastplate Jesus wore was impenetrable, and Satan could never pierce it because Jesus was totally righteous. He gives us this righteousness so we can also become impenetrable, affording us protection so we can live in perfect peace.

Jesus's feet were always ready to walk out the peace of the gospel and display its true power. Jesus's character was impeccable as He did exactly what the Father wanted Him to do. Walking the way God wanted Jesus to go was not always easy, but it was always the right thing to do. Jesus modeled the Christian life perfectly, and He extends this life to those who accept Him. His main mission on earth was to foil the antics of the devil by spreading the gospel and developing disciples who could carry on His efforts. By doing this, Jesus walked in victory, and if we follow His example, we shall overcome the troubles of this world as He did.

As He walked on this earth, Jesus displayed faith that was unlimited in measure. He could raise the dead, heal the sick, and cast out demons with a word. He performed every command given to Him by the Father with total obedience. Jesus has absolute trust in God, which is imparted to Him in the form of absolute power. Because of this power, the devil would never be able to get his fiery darts past the shield of Jesus. As we become more like Jesus, we can also build our faith to shield us from the antics of Satan.

The mind of Christ is a perfect mind and was once enjoyed by Adam and Eve. After the Fall, their minds became carnal and full of wickedness. The mind of Jesus is pure and untainted, which is totally guarded from the approach of the enemy. The helmet upon Jesus's head does not allow any ungodly thoughts to flourish, thus preventing any demonic stronghold from being formed. Jesus once stated the devil had nothing in Him (John 14:30), meaning Satan had no authority or legal claim to harass the Son of God. There is no battlefield in the mind of Christ, only peace and a true vision of what is right.

As mentioned previously, the sword of the Spirit can be used as a defensive and offensive tool. Jesus used the sword as a defensive weapon as illustrated in Mathew chapter 4. Using scripture, Jesus was able to neutralize every seduction of Satan. When Jesus returns, He will use the sword of the Spirit as an offensive weapon, for out of His mouth will come a sword that He will use to strike down the nations (Revelation 19:15). The Word of God is a vehicle that will make the whole world bow down to the Almighty. It is better for you to bow down willingly as a child of God than to be forced to do it as a nonbeliever condemned to eternal punishment.

The fight with the devil is on, and we are in the middle of the battle. You can free yourself from worry if you are a believer in Jesus because you fight from a position of victory. If God is on your side, nothing can stand against you (Romans 8:31). To be a soldier in God's army, we must act the part and be prepared to fight. Take your example from Jesus; put on your armor and raise your sword. The war has already been won!

CHAPTER 10

Love Conquers All

Love is patient, love is kind. It does not envy, it does not
boast, it is not proud. It is not rude, it is not self-seeking,
it is not easily angered, it keeps no record of wrong. Love
does not delight in evil but rejoices in the truth. It always
protects, always trusts, always hopes, always perseveres.
Love never fails.

—1 Corinthians 13:4–8

I once heard it preached if you replace the word love in the above
verses with the name of Jesus, the passage would be just as true.
God, Jesus, and the Holy Spirit are the embodiment of love. Reading
these verses may prompt one to perform a self-evaluation based on
the criteria outlined in the segment. If we call ourselves Christians,
then we should behave as God does, but we are not able to obtain
this perfection through ourselves. Luckily for us, Jesus is faithful and
true to forgive all our sins and cleanse us from all unrighteousness. (1
John 1:9). The only way to live in love is to live in Christ.

Love is an effective way to combat the devil and the self-centeredness that comes with our sin nature. To truly love, we must
think of others and not just feed our own agenda. Love is the power
of God, and the devil cannot understand it because love is totally
opposite of the characteristics that define evil. The devil is all about
self and has little concern for the welfare of others. Just as we have

a sinful nature born within us, God has also given us a measure of good.

Whatever you focus on is going to grow in your life. If your life is all about you, then your self-centered sin nature will be the dominate factor in your life. If you serve others, the seed of love God has planted in you will begin to blossom and will overtake self-centeredness. The more you serve, the more your capacity to love others will grow. When people serve God more than they serve themselves, the eyes of our hearts are opened wide to the greatness of our God. This is the last thing the devil wants to happen. He wants to keep you self-absorbed, which means focusing on you and your needs.

When children are young, the self-centered behavior can be observed in them. They may not want to share their toys with other children, or they may express jealousy when attention is taken away from them and given to someone else. It is through the instruction of good parents that children learn the importance of sharing and being considerate of others. Lack of disciplining the child allows a selfish adolescent to display the same behavior as an adult. Adults who grow up in this condition have a hard time relating to the feelings and needs of others because the seed of love has not flourished in them.

God commands us to love Him with all our mind, heart, strength, and soul (Luke 10:27). If you read over this passage too quickly, you may not realize the full ramifications of this verse. God is asking you to love Him with all your being, and He will not be happy with a small part of you because He desires all of you.

For some Christians, the full extent of their spiritual walk is to go to church on Sunday, but God does not want to see you only two hours a week. You cannot live for God one day a week and live like the world the rest of the time. God wants to have a relationship with you, which requires spending time together. If you only talked to your wife two hours a week, the marriage would not last very long. Without having a relationship with God, you will not know Him or understand His ways. Operating in the ways of God allows you to produce fruit consistent with His commands. Those who call God Lord but do not have a relationship with Him will hear these words when they meet Jesus: I never knew you (Matthew 7:23). This will be a sad day for those who have deceived themselves in this lifetime.

God dearly wants to have a relationship with you and be part of your life. This well-known passage is a testimony to that fact: "God so loved the world that He gave His only begotten Son, that whoever believes in Him should not perish but have everlasting life" (John 3:16). This is how much God values His creation. God loves you so much, He was willing to sacrifice His Son to free you from the punishment of sin. God's solution for sin is a free gift most people reject and ridicule. As great as God's love is for Jesus, He extended a greater love for you. Why? So He can be reunited with you for an eternity.

Who would sacrifice their own son for a bunch of people who did not even appreciate the effort? No one has ever known a greater love than Jesus has for you. Being a Christian means loving God and thanking Jesus for this sacrifice They have made for you. If God did not do another good thing in your life (which He will), He has already done enough. God also wants us to extend the love He has given us to other people.

And why should we love and bless others? Because Jesus values all people and wishes none would perish. This is why He died for us. If Jesus values everyone that much, then so should we. Loving your neighbor is respecting the value Jesus has for each and every person. To love your neighbor is to love God and appreciate His saving grace, the sacrifice of His Son.

Loving God and following His commandments are not always easy. Take the example of Mary, mother of Jesus, wife betrothed to her husband, Joseph. Mary was approached by the archangel Gabriel as he announced to her, "Rejoice highly favored one, the Lord is with you" (Luke 1:28). Then Gabriel foretold of God's plans to conceive a baby in Mary through the impregnation of the Holy Spirit (Luke 1:35).

Let's break down this situation and analyze it. God was indeed blessing Mary by choosing her to bear His Son. I know God was aware of how much Mary loved Him and her allegiance to be obedient to His calling. In the meeting with Gabriel, Mary's response to the request was, "Let it be to me according to your word" (Luke

1:38). In saying this, she was not thinking about herself or the potential hardships she may have to endure. Mary displayed a total trust in God to take care of any matter that would confront her.

This blessing, however, would present some problems in the young girl's life. Let's face it. Who would believe Mary was impregnated by the Holy Spirit? No one else witnessed the meeting between Mary and the archangel. People would have thought Mary had gone insane. This apparent infidelity would have caused her a multitude of serious issues. First, Mary being betrothed to Joseph and carrying a child that was not his was an offense that could have ended in divorce. Fortunately, God stepped in, and through an angelic dream, Joseph was told not to divorce Mary (Matthew 1:19–20). Secondly, her apparent adultery would have been a disgrace to her family, and they may have disowned her. Thirdly, being an unwed mother in biblical days was a serious infraction that was frowned upon. This misconstrued interpretation of Mary's condition may be the reason why she was not welcome into anyone's home during their visit to Bethlehem. Lastly, according to Hebrew law, Mary could have been stoned for her perceived misbehavior (Deuteronomy 22:20–24).

When we read about the virgin birth, we think about how blessed Mary was to be chosen by God for this event. As blessed as she was, you can see her service to God was not easy. Coming to Jesus does not mean every day is going to be sunshine and lollipops. Walking out God's plan for your life goes against the grain of this world's culture, and when you go against the grain, you eventually run into resistance. Looking at Mary's life through the eyes of reality, we can see her struggles and her total reliance on God. Can you imagine the pain Mary must have felt to witness her Son being beaten, ridiculed, and then crucified on the cross? But just like the situations that Mary encountered, God will also get you through your hardships while building your perseverance to make you stronger than before.

The story of the Prodigal Son is an excellent illustration of God's love for us (Luke 15:11–32). In this story, a father's younger of two sons requested his portion of the family's inheritance. After the father granted his son's request, the son takes his newfound wealth and moves to a foreign land, where he engages in a frivolous lifestyle. Once the money is depleted, the youngest son finds himself tending pigs as a means of employment. It is here at his lowest point the son ponders the wisdom of his father's ability to adequately care for his household. The son decides to return to the father and beg for his forgiveness in hopes of becoming one of his servants.

One of the first observations of this story is the arrogance of the son as he requests an inheritance before the passing of his father. His disrespect was further compounded by requesting his share before the elder son received his portion because the elder son was entitled to the first and largest portion of the estate. Secondly, the younger son had not yet achieved a level of maturity needed to be responsible for managing his finances. The young man had not yet gained the wisdom of the father, who obviously had been a wise steward of his resources in order to amass such great wealth. His father gave the younger son a great advantage he could have used to build a greater inheritance, but in his foolishness, he squanders his father's blessing.

On the return trip home, the father sees the son in the distance and runs to greet him. Before the son could get his confession out, the father orders a great celebration in honor of his son. The father in the story, who embraced his son with love, is a pale comparison as likened to how much God loves you. You cannot do anything so bad that God will not forgive you if you turn to Him. The wisdom of God surpasses man's reasoning, and God freely passes this wisdom to us in His Word. This is why it is important to know and follow His commands. He made His commands to protect us because He loves us that much. The inheritance God has given us is more important than any worldly inheritance could ever be. He has given us permission to share this inheritance with everyone who will accept the gift of salvation. Do not be like the foolish son but build on the inheritance God has given you and use it to grow the kingdom of God. This is how we serve God, a true reflection of our love for Him.

Those who do not accept Jesus are spiritually dead, but in Christ, you live. The wisdom of God is hidden from the lost by the blinders of this world. It is the job of the church to remove these blinders so unbelievers can see the truth. God displayed His love for you so you can love others. As you become more like God by loving more, revelation of who God is will become clearer to you. The world may breed hate, but love flows from the heart of God and those who are called by His name.

CHAPTER 11

Can You Hear Me?

Jesus spent His days performing the will of the Father and spent His nights praying to Him for direction. If Jesus found it necessary to spend this much time praying, how much more important is it for us to pray? Most Christians' prayer life is nonexistent. When we get in a tight spot or have nowhere else to turn, this is when the prayers flow freely. But God does not only want to hear from you when you are in trouble. He also wants to hear from you when things are going well. He delights in your success, and He lifts you up in your time of need. God's eyes are upon the righteous, and His ears hear our prayers (Psalm 34:15). Do not ever doubt that when you pray, God is listening to your request.

If God is truly listening, why does it seem our prayers go unanswered? There could be several reasons for this. When most people pray, they really don't believe God will answer their prayers. I have prayed for many people, and when I asked them if they thought God would answer their prayers, most replied, "I sure hope so." When you pray, you cannot just hope God is hearing your prayers, but you have to know He is hearing your prayers. In the book of James, it is written that if you doubt, you will not receive anything from the Lord (James 1:6–7). James goes as far as to call a doubting person unstable because you cannot be divided between belief and unbelief. God wants all of you, which include your total trust in Him. Without faith in God, it is impossible to please Him (Hebrews 11:6). Total faith equals total trust and God desires nothing less.

You may say, "I have faith God hears my prayers, and I believe He wants the very best for me, but my prayers still seem to go unanswered." Before His death, Jesus prayed so sincerely in the garden of Gethsemane, He bled blood out of His pores (Luke 22:39–46). I do not know about you, but I have never been that zealous in my prayer life. As sincerely as Jesus prayed for God to remove the cup from Him, Jesus also added this disclaimer: "Let your will be done" (verse 42). Sometimes it may not be in the will of God for your prayers to be answered as requested, but be assured, they will be answered. God's plan for your life is so much better than anything you could devise on your own, so be patient and wait for His plan to unfold.

Sometimes prayers go unanswered because God knows if He grants your request, it will create a greater gap between you and Him. For example, some people may pray for God to make them wealthy and famous. In the case of the rich young ruler (Luke 18:18–23), wealth had made it difficult for the rich man to have a relationship with Jesus. The rich man inquired and asked Jesus how he could obtain eternal life. When Jesus replied, "Sell all you have and give it to the poor, then follow Me" (verse 22), the rich man realized this request was too high of a price for him to pay. The truth was the rich man had made an idol out of his wealth, which was his focus of worship, leaving no room for Jesus in his life. That is not God's plan for your life, and He will not answer a prayer that will cause you to depart further from Him, your source of life.

Other prayers go unanswered because people are continually praying for themselves. God wants to bless you, but He does not want to inflate your carnal nature. Praying for a new car, a bigger house, or fancy clothing does little to build the kingdom of God. You were put on this planet to glorify God and spread the Word of salvation, not to feed your ego. Seek out God in your life and build His kingdom, and everything you need will be provided for you (Matthew 6:33). This does not mean God will not bless you with a new car or house, but these temporal items should not be your main prayer focus. By living for God and being a world changer, change will happen for you.

God can also use unanswered prayers to hone your character. In Isaiah 48:10, it states, "I have refined you, but not as silver; I have tested you in the furnace of affliction." When the trials come, we usually respond with, "God, get me out of this situation!" God may not be answering this prayer because He is using the tribulation to make you more like Him. There is nothing like a serious problem that makes you pause and think about your mortality. A cancer diagnosis can stop you in your tracks and make seeking God a top priority. After the situation has passed, you are now stronger than before and hopefully have a closer relationship with the Lord. If prayer for a hardship is not being answered, look for what God may be trying to change in you.

This is a fallen world, and Jesus has already warned us we will have trouble in this life (John 16:33). We do not have to worry because God is your refuge and strength, an ever-present help in times of trouble (Psalm 46:1). We should never be afraid to reach out to Him because God is love, and His concern for you is immense. It is through His strength we overcome the world, and His strength comes to us when we are on our knees in prayer.

Prayer is so important that Jesus gave us specific instructions on how to pray (Matthew 6:6–13). Jesus stated we should pray in private, in a secret place. Prayer is an intimate encounter between you and the God of the universe. It is a time when you release your heartfelt desires to God. God already knows what you need before you ask, so do not be afraid to come before Him with your request. Jesus even outlined a format for prayer;

> Our Father who art in heaven, hallowed be thy name, thy kingdom come, thy will be done on Earth as it is in Heaven. Give us this day our daily bread and forgive our trespasses as we forgive those who trespass against us. Lead us not into temptation, but deliver us from evil.

This prayer Jesus taught the apostles is an all-inclusive prayer meant to touch every aspect of our lives. Jesus, in His wisdom, was able to give us a prayer that is to the point, simple to remember, and a disruptive force to evil. Keep in mind this is not a bunch of words we repeat over and over again like a magic spell to propagate changes in our situations. It is a prayer we should say with meditation and deliberation, an emotionally stirring dialogue coming from our heart and touching the heart of God.

Further scrutiny of the prayer reveals its depth and different dimensions. By stating, "Our Father who art in Heaven," we are acknowledging Him as Almighty God who is willing and able to do all things. Because He is mighty and awesome, we hallow or honor His name, for He is holy. These first few phrases declare Him to be our spiritual Father worthy to be praised. This puts everything in the right order and perspective. Praising and worshipping God should always be the first priority in anything we do.

The next request in the prayer is that God's kingdom come and His will be done on earth. How do we make God's kingdom come to earth? This is done by seeking God and His righteousness continuously. Most of the time, we focus on building our own kingdom and doing what our will desires. We were put on this planet to do a specific mission, and this mission is to do the will of God. This means putting aside our dreams and worldly pursuits and making God the focal point of our existence.

God's ways are not our ways, and His direction sometimes does not seem to be logical. As always, we must trust in God and do what we sense He is instructing us to do. Only God can see the big picture, and one day, we will understand how these events fit together. This is the reason why prayer is so important. Through prayer, God gives us direction on the path we should follow. The more we pray, the better we are able to discern God's direction for us. We are the Lord's hands and feet here on earth, and His kingdom comes when Christians move in His will.

What are the benefits of having the will of God on earth as in heaven? In heaven, God the Father, Jesus the Son, and the Holy Spirit are in one accord, in perfect agreement, having one will and purpose. In this unity, the Godhead is able to do all things, and nothing is impossible for God (Luke 1:37). God is attracted to those who act in accordance to His commandments and do His will.

In Acts 2:1–4, it states the occupants in the upper room were of one accord, praying and seeking God. God honored their diligence, and the power of the Holy Spirit encompassed the room and filled the believers. This godly power allowed the apostles to preach, teach, and perform signs, miracles, and wonders. It was the power the apostles needed to start their ministry and the same power that is needed in ministries today.

God's kingdom on earth means having God's power with the ability to change society as we now know it. Imagine if thousands were suddenly saved, and people were miraculously healed of their diseases. This series of events could trigger a revival, causing believers to be of one accord, moving in the will of God. The Church would then be an unstoppable force.

The request for God to provide our daily bread shows we understand our provision comes from God. As mentioned before, you could not take your next breath unless God allowed you to do so. As humans, we tend to think everything we do is done in our own power, but our strength comes from God, and without Him, we cannot do anything.

If we cannot do anything without God's help, then we must be careful not to sever the power cord connecting us to Him. Having unrepented sin in your life can separate you from God. This is why it is important to ask Him to forgive our sins on a regular basis. If you are living in habitual sin, you are not in one accord with God but are living apart from Him. Living in sin states you know more than God about what is best for you. This is a condition of pride, the poison that separates you from God. When you repent (turn away) of your sin and ask for God's forgiveness, He is faithful to forgive your sin. It is a free gift from His Son Jesus, and all we have to do is accept this gift and relinquish our pride believing God knows what is best for us.

Equally important as it is to repent of our sins, we must also forgive those who sin against us. There once was a king who forgave a great debt of one of his servants (Matthew 18:23–35). This individual in turn went to a fellow servant and had him imprisoned because he owed him a small amount of money that he could not repay. When this report got back to the king, the servant who owed him a great deal of money was sent to the torturers until the debt could be paid. In verse 35, it states, this is what God will do to us if we do not forgive those who sin against us. Unforgiveness toward others not only blocks the blessing of God in your life but can cause you additional pain as you harbor this negative emotion in your heart.

Unforgiveness toward your neighbor is a serious offense. Like the man who owed the king a great debt, God forgave our debt through the sacrifice of His Son Jesus. And like the servant who had accrued this great debt, it is something we could never pay back. For this, we should be appreciative and have compassion on others as they trespass against us. Just as God has forgiven us, so we should also extend that grace to others.

Lastly, we ask God to help us fight the good fight by resisting temptation. The devil is always trying to tempt us, but God will give us the strength to resist temptation. When we are victorious over the snares of evil, we walk in a state of righteousness. Righteousness cannot come from what we have done, for all have sinned and fallen short of the glory of God (Romans 3:23). Only God is righteous, and only He can extend that quality to us. We can only fight evil when we allow God to be our shield in the heat of the battle.

God is a God of relationships, and the only way to build a strong relationship is through communication. Prayer is the communication tool needed to build a strong bond with God. The more that you pray, the more you will sense the presence of God and His direction for your life. God is listening, and He delights in talking with you. Make it a point to have a conversation with your Creator today.

CHAPTER 12

Faith Walk

We walk by faith, not by sight.

—2 Corinthians 5:7

In the Scriptures, there is a story of Jesus walking on the water as the apostles navigated their boat on the wave tossed Sea of Galilee (Matthew 14:22–33). When the apostle first observed Jesus performing this supernatural act, they were full of fear, but Jesus comforted them with a greeting. Marveling at Jesus's ability to stroll on top of the waves, Peter requested permission to do the same. Jesus invited Peter to join Him, an invitation Peter eagerly received as he climbed out of the boat and began his faith walk.

At the beginning, all is well, and Peter is operating in the realm of the supernatural as he focuses on Jesus. Keep in mind the storm was still brewing when Peter steps out of the boat, but he successfully walks upon the rough seas. Peter's downfall comes when he shifts his attention to the wind and the waves, an action that displaces his ability to stay above the water. With this, he begins to sink into despair, crying out for Jesus to save him.

We may be quick to judge Peter for his lack of faith, but one thing we must realize is he had enough faith to get out of the boat. There were eleven other apostles with Peter who did not volunteer to leave the confines of the vessel. The other apostles chose the natural security of the boat instead of opting for the supernatural interaction with their Lord and Master. Walking with God is always a choice.

As Christians, most of us are a lot like the eleven apostles who stayed in the boat. We find comfort in the tangible items we can see and touch while not experiencing the miraculous provision of God. Many Christians say they believe in the power of God, but when it comes time to step out, they are afraid to leave their comfort zone. When you walk with Jesus, you do not have to be afraid to take a risk. Did He not pull Peter out of the consuming waves? The Lord is with us and will never forsake us (Deuteronomy 31:6), so don't be afraid to step out of your place of security. Jesus sometimes allows the storms so you can journey from the comfort of this natural life into a supernatural existence with Him.

Look at the Bible heroes in Hebrews chapter 11 who excelled in their faith. Abraham left his homeland for a foreign land he did not know, believing in God's promise to make his lineage into a great nation (verses 8–9). Abraham was prepared to offer his son as a sacrifice per God's instructions, concluding that God would raise him from the dead (verses 17–19). Moses refused to live a life of royalty and chose to lead the Israelites following God's direction (verses 23–25). By faith, the Israelites marched around the city of Jericho seven times until the walls fell (verse 30). Over and over, we can see when people have faith in God's power, they can overcome seemingly impossible obstacles. Jesus said, "If you have faith as small as a mustard seed, you can say to this mountain, move and it will move" (Matthew 17:20). That is a lot of power for a little bit of faith. What mountain are you trying to move? Is it sickness, financial or relationship problems? Speak to that mountain with faith and watch it move with the power of Christ Jesus.

By using this experience of walking on the water, Jesus was trying to convey a very important concept to Peter and the apostles. Jesus never promised us a trouble-free life, and bad situations will eventually find you, but God has given us the ability to withstand any problem. The Holy Spirit ensured Jesus was walking over the water during the storm no matter how high the waves became. Jesus trusted the Father for His provision and protection against life's troubles. Just like Jesus, we can overcome the storms through Christ who strengthens us (Philippians 4:13). Besides, the storms do not last forever, and these tribulations should increase your spiritual strength, bringing you closer to God.

The devil will always try to break your focus off of Jesus by introducing some kind of turbulence into your life. If Satan can distract you through the use of hardship, he can keep you from walking in freedom. The last thing Satan wanted Peter to do was to keep successfully walking on the water, so he broke Peter's concentration using the storm. Let us imagine Peter kept his focus on Jesus and continued to walk on the water in spite of the wind and the waves. Remember, there were eleven other apostles watching from the safety of the boat. If Peter continued to walk on the water, the other apostles might start thinking, *If Peter can do this, so can I.*

Before long, all the apostles would be dancing on the waves ignoring the storm. The apostles could then demonstrate to others how to focus on Jesus and operate in the supernatural. This situation would have the potential to spread like a wildfire, preventing the devil from being able to contain it, while losing his demonic control over people.

If faith is so powerful, why do we not experience supernatural events regularly? In order to witness the supernatural, you must possess faith and also action. Faith without works is dead (James 2:26). For Peter to walk on the water, he first had to get out of the boat. Jesus invited Peter onto the sea, but Peter had to decide to accept the offer and then follow through with action. The walls of Jericho would have not fallen if the Israelites did obey God's command to march around the city seven times. This involves more than just getting out of your comfort zone, it requires total trust in God.

Let's use an example of a traffic light to illustrate the concept. When you approach a green light, you travel through the intersection having full faith that the lights in the other directions are red. We trust the technology so much, we never slow down or even give a second thought about the possibility of the traffic light having a malfunction. If we can trust our lives to man-made instruments, how much more should we trust God? When God told Abraham to travel to a foreign land, he saw God's green light, and he moved. Through this undying faith, God blessed Abraham despite his mistakes, and he will do the same for you. If you believe God is telling you to move, first pray about it and check to see if the direction lines up with God's Word. If you are still unsure, then seek wise counsel from a pastor or mature believers. If everything is in agreement, pray for the Holy Spirit to give you guidance and start your faith walk.

Many Christians believe once you say the prayer of salvation, the next step is to wait for death then go to heaven. By doing this, people miss out on the glorious life God wants them to experience. The Christian life was not meant to be a boring existence but an exciting power-filled life that consists of living free from the bondage of fear in the embrace of pure faith. Christians who operate in faith are people who overcome impossible odds to build the kingdom of God. They triumph over all obstacles by the power of the Holy Spirit.

Faith allows you to see trouble for what it really is: resistance caused by the evil one. This resistance is designed to discourage you, but pushing back against the resistance allows you to build spiritual muscle, thus expanding your faith. The more we push, the stronger we get. As you keep pushing back against the devil, you will be strong enough to navigate through any trial he throws at you.

For me, there is no testament to faith more touching than the story of the two criminals crucified with Jesus (Luke 23:39–43). In this encounter, one of the thieves is taunting Jesus while the three were being crucified. This thief wants to be free from his punishment to return to the wicked life he was living. The second thief comes to Jesus's defense, commenting that He did not deserve punishment because He had done nothing wrong. This second thief realized the punishment he was receiving was justified and was truly sorry for the crimes he had committed. The second man's regret becomes obvious when he asked Jesus to remember him when He came into His kingdom. Jesus then replies, "Today you will be with me in paradise" (verse 43). This second man displayed his faith in Jesus and it was confirmed with a reservation in heaven.

While the second man surrendered his life to Jesus, the first thief was blinded to salvation because his faith was in what the world could offer. The things of this world will pass away, and you cannot take them with you. Putting your faith in the world is foolishness, so put your faith in the Lord and He will show you grace.

God made us to step on the prince of this world, but we cannot defeat the devil in our own strength. The devil is too cunning and will overpower you if you trade punches with him. Your only hope is having faith in God and the power of His Spirit to combat the enemy. Faith in the Lord is the only path to victory.

CHAPTER 13

Religion Is Not Relationship

God created mankind because He wanted to have a relationship with humanity. That's why God visited Adam and Eve in the garden during the cool of the day as described in Genesis chapter 3. The God of the universe took time out of His day to fellowship with humans. How awesome is that! And since we know that God is love (1 John 4:8), I am willing to bet these interactions were the best part of His day.

As it was in the days of Eden, so it should be today. God's character has not changed, and He delights in interacting with you. He already knows everything about you: what your good points are and what you have done wrong, but He still loves you. Unfortunately, most Christians do not grasp this very important concept. They go through the motions of going to church, reading their Bibles, and doing good deeds but do not have a personal relationship with God. Following the rules without love for God is called religion.

Religion is based on man-made doctrine that governs the actions of people to seem pious but does not have anything to do with serving God. Religion states if you follow the strict code of ethics, you are a good person bound for heaven. This is a works-based philosophy, not a God-based theology that extends salvation to anyone who accepts it as a free gift. Jesus rebuked the Pharisees for following the letter of the law by doing something insignificant as tithing on their spices but neglecting important matters like mercy and justice (Matthew

23:23). Religion is driven by following the rules, while relationship is motivated by matters of the heart.

The problem with religion is we cannot follow the law perfectly enough to get into heaven. That is why God devised the plan of sacrificing His Son. If we accept Jesus as Lord of our lives, He will set us free from sin, and we will inherit eternal life with Him.

The importance of relationships is clearly demonstrated by Jesus as He performed His ministry here on earth. In everything He did, Jesus would pray to the Father for direction and power to perform the task. Jesus never glorified Himself but always gave glory to God. In His relationships with people, Jesus was always quick to heal their sicknesses and tend to their needs. You can witness the humility in the actions of Jesus displayed throughout His life on this planet. It was never about Jesus; it was always about the Father. Jesus even stated He only does what He sees the Father doing (John 5:19). Jesus loved God and us so much that He gave His life so we would not perish.

In most human relationships, people are always looking for what they can get out of the partnership. I believe marriages would have a higher success rate if people focused on how they could first serve God then their spouse. As Jesus glorified God, God in turn glorified His Son. There is no self-centeredness in love, only service and dying to one's carnal nature. If you truly love someone, this is the posture you should exhibit in your relationships. Of course, nobody is perfect, and growing in love is a process, not a destination.

The process of growing in love can be seen in the relationship of the apostles with Jesus. At first, the apostles were excited to be picked by Jesus to be His disciples, but their hearts were not totally surrendered to Him. I believe they loved Jesus, but there was also a lot of self-centeredness in the beginning of the relationship. The apostles were looking to see how their friendship with Jesus could benefit them. They argued among themselves about who was going to be the greatest (Mark 9:34), a clear sign of pride. Jesus tried to explain to them that the one who is the greatest is the one who is a servant to all. The apostles must have not quite grasped the concept because a short while later, James and John asked if they could sit in places of honor on His right and left side. Religion embellishes pride, while relationship stems from humility. In the beginning, the pride of the apostles can be clearly observed.

When did the apostles surrender themselves and give their hearts to Jesus? When they did what Jesus told them to do: serve. In the upper room at Pentecost, they were all of one accord, not arguing about who the greatest was but focusing on the Greatest. After they were filled with the Holy Spirit, believers sold their possessions and gave to those who were in need (Acts 2:45). They had made the transition love brings—from selfishness to selflessness. Peter, who had once betrayed Jesus, chose death instead of denouncing His name. Most of the apostles experienced agonizing deaths instead of denying the existence of Jesus. The apostles made the full metamorphosis from religion to relationship by giving their all to God.

To get a true picture of what religion looks like, we can observe the actions of the Pharisees and the Sadducees. This religious council took the Ten Commandments and expounded upon them to create hundreds of rules and regulations they enforced the people to follow. This list of rules complicated the process of serving God and made it an impossible feat. Jesus took the Ten Commandments and simplified them because His motivation is relationship, not religion. Jesus proclaimed we should love the Lord our God and our neighbor as ourselves. He also said that these very principles satisfy the law and the prophets. In other words, all the commandments in the Bible are fulfilled by loving God and each other. Jesus could see right through the hypocrisy of the members of the religious council and called them whitewashed tombs full of dead men's bones (Matthew 23:27). On the outside, the Pharisee and Sadducees appeared to be holy, but their hearts were unclean and filled with wickedness.

The religious spirit can also be observed in the behavior of the Pharisee of Pharisees. Paul was educated by one of the most prominent rabbis and had accumulated an abundance of head knowledge but lacked in the area concerning matters of the heart. Paul was persecuting God's people, thinking he was doing the Lord a service, but this all changed when he met Jesus on the road to Damascus (Acts 9:1–19). The spirit of religion and carnality blinded Paul from knowing the one true God, but the Holy Spirit opened the eyes of Paul, graduating him from religion to relationship. No longer was Paul full of pride over his accomplishments but full of love for the Lord God. Paul used the rest of his life to serve God and suffered much for his allegiance.

Serving God is not a part-time proposition but a full-time commitment. God desires all of you, not just a small portion of your life. The devil does not mind you going to church or reading your Bible as long as you do not make a connection to the Lord of lords. Many churches today are void of the power of the Holy Spirit because they are not fully surrendered to God. When the body of Christ mixes with the culture of the world, it dilutes Christianity, making us lukewarm. Jesus said He would vomit a lukewarm church out of His mouth (Revelation 3:16). Serving God means to be untainted by the matters of the world and focused on our relationship with Him.

The spirit of religion is full of empty promises, but it is only through relationship that promises can reach fruition. Religion states if you are good enough, you are guaranteed a spot in heaven. Without Jesus, a lot of good people who think they are going to heaven are actually going to go to hell. Only the blood of Jesus can wash you clean of your sins, making you righteous and heaven bound. This is part of God's inheritance for His children, and you cannot take part in it if you are not a member of the family. Only those who accept and know Jesus will ascend into the presence of Father God. No person is good enough to get to heaven without Jesus.

Also, with relationship comes authority. Sons and daughters of God know their Father's business and act for the betterment of the kingdom. Children who have the Father's best interest at heart are given a measure of authority. This is the authority Jesus spoke of over all the power of darkness (Luke 10:19).

In Acts 16:18, it speaks how Paul was able to use this authority to cast a demon out of a slave girl through the power of God. When the sons of Sceva tried to use this authority to cast out an evil spirit, they were severely beaten by the demon (Acts 19:13–16). The spirit knew about the authority Jesus and Paul had but did not see any power or legal right in the relatives of Sceva to command him out of the person. A deputy only has authority to uphold the law when they are in relationship with the sheriff and have been appointed that right. Without the appointment, a person has no authorization to enforce the law. Paul, being a child of God, was anointed with godly authority, an authority the sons of Sceva did not possess.

Many churches today are operating without God's authority, a condition that makes them of little consequence against the evil of this world. Authority over Satan is only achieved through a relationship with the one true God, the Lord Jesus Christ.

With relationship, there is also a transfer of power. A son of a prominent father is treated a lot differently than a regular person. For example, the son of the president of the United States commands a greater amount of respect as compared to the son of a common man. This respect does not come from anything the son has done but is a reflection of the father's position. Your Father is the Lord of lords, and no one is more prominent than Him, which, by default, makes believers the King's kids.

When you are in relationship with God, not only do you have the authority or legal right over evil, you have the power to subdue it. When the devil sees you, he really sees the seal of Jesus that has washed you clean of your sins. Satan recognizes the authority of Jesus you carry and will obey the Word of God that comes forth from you. The power does not come from anything you have done but from the blood of Jesus and the power of the Holy Spirit working through you. As sons and daughters of the Most High, we are to use this authority and power in a way that aligns with our Father's commandments. By operating in this fashion, we glorify God and expand His kingdom.

God always measures a person by their capacity to love. When God sent the prophet Samuel to the house of Jesse to anoint the next king of Israel, He did not pick the candidate based on his physical appearance. Though the seven eldest sons paraded by Samuel displayed admirable features, God chose the eighth and youngest son, David, because his heart was pure (1 Samuel 16:1–13). God is not impressed with how good looking you are or how strong you are, but He is concerned with how compassionate you are. So if you have not been blessed with an impressive physical stature, do not count yourself out of God's service. God is not searching for what the world esteems but for anyone who is pliable and is ready to be used by Him. Fame in this world does not equate to glory in heaven. The people who have served God without their actions being recognized by men will be greatly honored in heaven. So in all that you do, do it unto the Lord and not for the praises of men (Colossians 3:23) because the Lord God always sees what His children do in secret.

Your service to God will be hindered if your feet are firmly planted in religion. The apostles were not very effective ministers when they were looking to exalt themselves but excelled when they began to exalt God. Paul was of no benefit to the kingdom of God when he was persecuting Christians, but when his eyes were opened, God worked through him mightily. God can do the same with you if you keep your focus on Him and not on what the world thinks. He effectively uses those whose hearts are right with Him.

CHAPTER 14

Put It into Practice

Jesus said, "The one who follows my commandments is like the one who built his house upon the rock" (Matthew 7:24). God's Word is wisdom to be used to keep us out of the snares of the evil one. Trouble will surely come to you in this lifetime, but those who stand on God's Word can weather the storm. The rock we build our foundation upon should be none other than Christ Jesus. No matter how violent the storm gets, the devil cannot undermine the bedrock of Christ. Tribulations will come, and they will go, but you do not have to be afraid if you are practicing biblical truths.

Most Christians wonder why their lives are so full of turmoil even though they seem to be doing everything right. Many go to church every Sunday and occasionally read their Bibles, but few are living the life God intended them to have. Although they heard the sermon the pastor preached on Sunday morning, most Christians cannot remember the content of the message an hour after the church service, never mind applying the concepts to their daily existence. The Bible may seem like an easy-reading book filled with good stories, but it is sound doctrine that should be used by God's people. Those who do not practice the biblical lifestyle are compared to a person whose foundation is built upon the sand (Matthew 7:26). The storms we encounter can easily wash away the sand, and when it does, there is only destruction left. This condition affects Christians and nonbelievers alike.

In addition, those who do not put the words of Jesus into action are by default people who practice lawlessness (Matthew 7:23). When you ponder on it, if you are not doing what God instructs you to do, then you are living like the world. Some of these worldly practices include fornication, idolatry, adultery, homosexuality, thievery, covertness, drunkenness, and revelry (1 Corinthians 6:9–10). World values are contrary to the holy ways of God, and living the principles of this world is basically living apart from God. We are not to be conformed to this world but transformed to the image of Christ. When Jesus returns, He will be looking for His faithful ones. Don't allow this day to catch you off guard.

So how do we live a life pleasing to God and useful for His service? This can be accomplished by studying the life of Jesus, for He is the master of godly living. When we observe the actions of Jesus during His ministry here on earth, we have a pattern to replicate so we can live as He did. Jesus is an excellent model of right living, so let's examine His life and see how we can apply it to our own.

First and foremost, Jesus loves Father God with all His being and lives out this most important commandment (Matthew 22:37). During His earthly ministry, Jesus was in continuous communication with the Father by engrossing Himself in constant prayer. Not only did Jesus pray, but He acted upon what the Father required Him to do. Proverbs 13:1 states, "A wise son heeds his father's instruction," and Jesus obeyed this proverb in the strictest sense.

A good father has compiled a great deal of wisdom during his lifetime, and it is his greatest wish to share this knowledge with his children. Most parents want only good things for their children, and so does God. Following the wisdom of God is a sure way to a better life. Jesus was a good Son who followed His Father's instruction to His death. Without Jesus's obedience to the Father, we would have died in our sins, living in eternal damnation. Loving God and being obedient to His Word are the cornerstone to living right.

Being obedient to God's Words can sometimes be difficult. Put yourself in Noah's place when God asked him to build the ark because He was going to destroy life on earth with a great flood (Genesis 6–8). The ark itself was approximately 450 feet long, the length of a medium-size cruise ship. This ark was to be fabricated by hand in a period absent of heavy construction equipment and machinery. Then after completing the project, Noah was commanded to collect up all the animals and the food needed to sustain them. This seems like an impossible task even in this day of modern technology.

To add the icing on the cake, people of Noah's day must have thought that he was crazy because before the flood, it had never rained. Imagine the ridicule Noah had to endure while he was doing what God had asked him to do. But following God's instructions allowed Noah and his family to survive when the flood did come. God supplied Noah with the strength, resources, and knowledge to accomplish this gigantic task. God sometimes gives you a task that is bigger than you so He can display His great might. If you obey God, He will not let you fail and will supply you with all you need to honor Him. Following God is not always the easiest choice, but it is always the right one.

Jesus was also focused on discipling others in the ways of God. He was constantly sharing the gospel (which means "good news") so people would know about God's grace. After people were converted, Jesus also went a step further and gave new followers additional instruction so they could walk out their newfound lifestyle. Most Christians today are afraid to share their faith for fear of being ridiculed. If you step out and share your faith, people may mock you, for the ways of the world are different from the ways of the Father. But Christians are called to suffer and bear their crosses so others can be exposed to the truth. Besides, how great is our suffering as compared to the pain Jesus went through to pay for our sins? If your efforts save one person, the price for your suffering would be well worth it.

God desires that nobody perishes in hell but for all to be saved (accept Jesus) so they can spend an eternity with Him. Once people are saved, making disciples out of these new converts is godly wisdom, for the more disciples you train, the more people you have to reach the lost. Making disciples is not just the pastor's job either; it requires the whole body of believers.

When it comes to the matters of truth and justice, Jesus is bold. This zeal can be witnessed when Jesus chased the moneylenders out of the temple (John 2:13–16). The temple was a place of worship, not a marketplace for making profit. Jesus stood up for what was right no matter what the potential consequences would be. Even when religious leaders were trying to make Him stumble, Jesus did not back down. When the priests and the scribes doubted His authority (Luke 20:1–8), Jesus posed this question to them: "Was John's baptism from heaven or from men?" The leaders spoke among themselves weighing their options. If they responded that this proclamation was from heaven, they would have to agree with John's words acknowledging the divinity of Jesus. If they stated John the Baptist made up the conclusion about Jesus's divinity, the people would turn on them because they honored John as a prophet. Being trapped in this no-win situation caused the leaders to refuse to answer the question. Jesus gave the priests an opportunity to declare the truth, but they refused to humble themselves to the Lord and Master. Jesus was bold and did not fear their authority, for He is the ultimate authority. He therefore refused to justify Himself by answering the religious leaders' question.

We are called to be the light in this fallen world and to stand against injustices that conflict with the truth. This boldness comes by allowing the Holy Spirit to rule and reign in your life. Giving the Holy Spirit freedom to work through you and conquer the strongholds of Satan is the mark of a true believer. There is always a price to pay when you follow in the footsteps of Jesus, and this practice will always produce resistance from the world's culture. Apostle Paul knew of the hardships of serving God firsthand as he faced beatings, tribulations, and prison time, but the impressions his work left are still shaping the world today. We are called to be world changers, but we must walk in the Spirit of boldness while fighting against the evil residing in this world.

Jesus possesses a very important quality, which is wisdom. No matter how many times the Pharisees tried to make Jesus say something incriminating, He always turned the tables on them. When the Pharisees and the Herodians questioned Jesus about whether it was lawful to pay taxes to the Roman Empire (Mark 12:14), Jesus discerned that He was being baited. If Jesus replied it was wrong to pay taxes, the Herodians, who supported Caesar's policies, would have accused Him of treason. On the other hand, if Jesus acknowledged it was right to pay taxes, the Pharisees would have made Him out to be an enemy of Israel, for the Israelites despised Roman rule.

Just when the Pharisees and the Herodians thought they had caught Jesus in an ironclad trap, Jesus responds brilliantly. Jesus asked for a Roman coin and inquired whose picture was depicted on the coin. The crowd responded, "Caesar!" and with that, Jesus said, "Give to Caesar what is Caesar's and give to God things that are God's" (Mark 12:17). Jesus outwitted His opponents by using godly wisdom.

In this world, wisdom is needed to combat the foolishness of this generation. Many proponents of false doctrine think they have discovered the secret to eternal life, but they are just false prophets leading others away from God with their dribble. Wisdom always defeats the worldly culture and neutralizes its destructive effects. To obtain wisdom, Proverbs 1:7 states, "the fear of the Lord is the beginning of knowledge." Without fear or reverence for God, obtaining wisdom from the Holy Spirit would be impossible, but building a relationship with God makes all things possible. To walk in this time without the wisdom of God is a dangerous prospect. Having knowledge of God's Word is a crucial component in your defense against the devil, so grow closer to God and live out His Word so you will be able to easily spot the truth.

Lastly, Jesus is humble and has a servant's heart. I sometimes find it hard to imagine that the God of the universe has such a great compassion for people whom He spent His ministry here on earth serving. It blows my mind that Jesus, who is fully God, is totally concerned about our welfare. His love was genuine as He reached out and healed the sick, cast out demons, and raised the dead. His attitude is one of gentle correction without condemnation for those who are diligently seeking Him. Jesus is the epitome of love, truly possessing a servant's posture.

As humans, understanding the role of a servant may be one of the hardest concepts to master. Even after Jesus told His disciples the greatest among them would be the one who served others

(Matthew 23:11), the apostles did not take immediate heed of this message. They continued to jockey for positions of power in what they thought was going to be the earthy kingdom. To be great is to be like Jesus, and that is what we should be doing with our time here in this world. We will fall short of the mark, but as we grow closer in relationship with God, He will grow closer to us. Having great material possessions or a position of power pales in comparison to the glory of Christ Jesus, so continue to seek Him out and conform to His image. In doing so, you will be called great in the kingdom of heaven.

Jesus, being the perfect man, has many more remarkable qualities, which would probably take a lifetime to review. With that being said, if you love God and are obedient to His calling with boldness and in wisdom, you will be successful in living out God's commission. And always remember, the Holy Spirit will guide us and help us stay on the path of righteousness as we battle against evil. Living out God's Word is what life was meant to be.

CHAPTER 15

The Temple

In the Old Testament times, there was a multitude of various gods people worshipped. Temples were built by these ancient civilizations so they could pay homage to these idols, conducting worship services held in their honor. For example, the Canaanites venerated Baal, who they believed was the god of fertility. The Philistines revered Dagon, who was supposedly the father of Baal. In the rituals honoring the god Moloch, child sacrifices were practiced to invoke his favor. Many pagan worship services involved sexual practices between the congregation and the priests/priestesses. Temples were often elaborate in their construction, displaying the great respect worshippers had for the gods of their choosing.

The Jewish people glorified the one true God and built a temple to serve and honor Him. The Jewish sanctuary was different from the pagan shrines because the Spirit of God dwelled among His people. The power of the Lord God was tangible with His manifest presence saturating the structure. This manifestation of God occurred in a special location of the temple called the holy of holies, a place where the priests were only allowed to enter once a year on Yom Kippur. During this day, the high priest of Israel would proceed into the holy of holies to atone for the sins of the nation. This was a serious practice that could potentially cost the priest his life. The presence of God was so powerful that if the sins of the high priest were not properly cleansed, he would die instantly. Sin does not have a chance when exposed to the glory of God.

When you mention the word *temple*, a lot of people think of a church building, but that does not always have to be the case. Let's define what a temple is. A temple is the residence of a god or God one chooses to worship and serve. For the pagans, these gods included the ones mentioned above and many others. These were man-made gods created to serve their needs and were housed in buildings of great grandeur built by the hands of man.

For Christians, there is only one God, the Lord Jesus Christ, and He no longer dwells in a temple built by man. Paul stated Christians are the temple of God and that the Holy Spirit dwells within us (1 Corinthians 3:16). Basically, Christians are a resting place resembling the holy of holies! Not only is this an awesome revelation but also a great responsibility. Knowing we are the temple of God and that His Spirit lives in us, we should try to live our lives by being holy and righteous to reflect the God we serve. If an important person like the queen of England was going to visit your home, you would probably tidy the place up a little. If you would do this for human royalty, how much more important is it to prepare your temple for heavenly royalty.

For this reason, a Christian's perspective should be different than the world's view, but most of the time, this is not the case. As humans, we tend to spend a majority of our time watching mindless television that portrays concepts contrary to the ways of God. Almost all entertainment today—such as video games, social media, and movies—are not God honoring. If you watch, listen, or practice activities that are not in alignment with godly principles, you are filling your temple with garbage.

Can you image going to church on Sunday and finding the building torn apart and filled with trash? This would probably be a shock to most people, but this is exactly what we do when we act outside of the character of God. When this happens, we must follow the example set by King Hezekiah. Before King Hezekiah's reign, the Israelites had turned their backs on the Lord and let the temple suffer disrepair. The Bible states the doors were busted down, and the temple was filled with rubbish (2 Chronicles 29:3–5). The Israelites no longer honored God or took the time to worship Him, defiling the temple with pagan artifacts. One of the first acts King Hezekiah performed when he took office was to cleanse the temple and set it in order.

Like Hezekiah, we must cleanse our temple and make it a suitable dwelling place for the Holy Spirit. We must stop desecrating ourselves by what we do, watch, and or listen to. This can be accomplished by asking the Holy Spirit to help guide our behavior to live a righteous life. For those instances when we fail to do so, we ask Jesus to forgive our sins, and He will wash us clean. For those who are unsaved, accepting Jesus is the first step in their journey because only the blood of Jesus can remove the sins from your temple.

I once knew a young man who said when he cleaned up his life, he would start attending church. Sadly, the man died in a motorcycle accident before he came to the revelation that only Jesus can forgive sin. If you could clean up your own sins, you would not need Jesus. Accepting Jesus's offer of salvation is not something you should put off for another day. You never know what day may be your last, so ask Jesus to forgive you of your sin and then repent or turn away from any evil practice. Remember, sin does not stand a chance in the presence of the glory of God. Temple cleansing is a lifelong process, but the grace of God is more than able to remove all sin out of your life.

Our sanctification allows us to be more sensitive to the Holy Spirit. The more refuse we get out of our temple, the more our sensitivity increases. The indwelling of the Holy Spirit may seem like a strange concept to most Christians, but it should be one of the most natural experiences we have. He is not there to control you but to guide you to the path of righteousness. We must work with the Holy Spirit and allow Him to teach us how to have a closer relationship with Him.

Sadly, most Christians will never experience the power of the Holy Spirit in their lives due to the amount of baggage they have accumulated. The Holy Spirit is not going to compete with the worries and pleasures of this world. His still, small voice will be drowned out by the chaos of worldly matters. The Holy Spirit will not force

Himself on you. Christians must choose to clear their minds and hearts from temporal affairs, choosing to listen to the Spirit of God instead. The Holy Spirit is a gift from God given to you for direction, instruction, and power. To refuse this help is like refusing a guaranteed victory against evil.

So how do you know when you are successfully purifying your temple? You can tell the condition of your temple by observing if there is any change in your attitude. Jesus said you can determine the character of someone by the fruit they produce (Matthew 7:16–20). If there is no change in your life and you are doing the same activities as non-Christians, then you are not producing godly fruit. People who are just pursuing pleasure and focusing their attention on themselves are self-seeking and filled with selfish ambition. This is not the way to serve Christ. People who practice this type of lifestyle need to examine their relationship and commitment to God. If you are a Christian, the Holy Spirit will convict you of wrongdoing and show you the correct way to live. As you walk in this lifestyle and become mature, you will become more like Christ. If you are not a Christian, accepting the Lord Jesus Christ is the only way to salvation that produces a godly existence.

On the other hand, those who give praise and glorify God in every situation are believers producing fruit consistent with biblical truths. Building the kingdom of God is done through selfless actions. Those who serve and build up others without any concern for what they may receive in return do the will of the Father. To perform the will of God, you must be God focused, not focusing on fulfilling your own desires. Truly loving God and being in relationship with Him are the only true ways to obtain a God-focused posture.

An illustration of a transition to being God focused can be observed in the lives of the apostles. The apostles were chosen by Jesus, and maybe with the exception of Judas, I believe that they all turned out to be God-fearing believers. In the beginning, the apostles were immature and were looking to bring glory to themselves. They spent their time seeking to outdo each other and establish a pecking order to determine their positions in Jesus's kingdom, which they surmised would be an earthly domain. Their main motivation was about who was going to be the greatest among them (Luke 9:46).

The real change in the apostles can be seen after Jesus is crucified, leaving them without their leader. The apostles went into seclusion to wait on the coming of the Holy Spirit just as Jesus had promised. In the days before Pentecost, the apostles were praying and were of one heart and mind. This is a totally different posture from their earlier actions when they were in competition with one another. This was a time of preparation for the arrival of the Holy Spirit. Being in one accord demonstrates the absence of the carnal nature, a transition into godly harmony.

As the apostles matured and cleansed themselves from their selfish desires, they created an inviting abode for the Holy Spirit. On the day of Pentecost, the apostles received an infilling of God's Spirit and spent the rest of their time on earth glorifying God and pointing all the attention toward Him. The conversion from selfishness to selflessness can be clearly discerned in this application.

Understanding a little bit about Jewish wedding customs also clearly signifies the importance of why we should be shaping ourselves to be more like God. The Jewish wedding ritual begins with a visit from the man to the home of his love interest. The man then propositions the woman with a proposal of marriage, and if she accepts, a covenant is made between them. At this stage, the man and woman are now betrothed. The man then leaves to build a home for his new bride, while the woman eagerly awaits his return.

During her time of waiting, she prepares herself to be presentable to her future husband. She does not worry about her current accommodations because she knows this is not going to be her permanent residence. The bride is not sure when the groom will return, but she wants to be ready to leave her old life behind and start a brand-new one with him. She diligently tries to align herself to complement her husband by becoming more like him. Once the groom completes his work, he then goes to the bride to be united with her in an official ceremony.

As with the Jewish tradition, Jesus left heaven and came to earth to visit His bride (Christians). Jesus proposes a spiritual joining to Him in which the promise of eternal life is made. If we accept the proposal, we are now betrothed to Jesus, and He has gone and prepared a place for us (John 14:2–3). This is the period in time where Christians are now. We are waiting for the return of the groom (second coming of Jesus) to take us to our new home (heaven). While we are waiting, we must make ourselves ready for the groom. This is not accomplished by buying a bigger house, a more expensive car, or fancier clothing but by following the commandments of Jesus and making ourselves more like Him. We should not worry about our present situation because this is only our temporary home. The eternal home of a true believer is in heaven with the Lord Jesus Christ. Though we may not all be alive at the second coming of Jesus, the preparation for His arrival should continue to our deaths.

If we were truly preparing for His return, the Church would look a lot more like Jesus. Regrettably, most people are more concerned about their present living conditions than their future in eternity. Christians are called to be the bride of Christ (Revelation 19:7), with the Lord being our groom at the wedding supper of the Lamb. This marriage can only happen when the Church (body of believers) is described as being holy and without blemish (Ephesians 5:27). Looking at the Church today, it is a fair statement to say we have not attained this level of purity, so believers have to start doing their part by turning their attention to God and sweeping their temples clean! As God is holy, we should be holy as well.

Why is this reformation of the body of believers so important? Christians are called to be the light of the world through Christ Jesus. The main purpose of the Church is to serve others and make disciples. Many people are living in darkness and do not understand the sacrifice Jesus made for all people. The temple of the unsaved is not the home of the Holy Spirit but may be a dwelling place for demons. These demonic tenants will try to fill people with all kinds of ungodly desires to secure their allegiance with the dark side. A temple filled with darkness will struggle to see the light of salvation. To people in this condition, the power of the cross may seem like foolishness (1 Corinthians 1:18), and their ability to digest the wisdom of the Scriptures is greatly hindered.

To shine the light into these people's lives, the Church needs to have their house in order. As long as the Church acts like the world, it will be void of power and the capacity to lead souls to Jesus. For Christians, cleansing of our inner temples is a must to allow the Spirit to flow through us and use us to change the world. God's children are called to win the world for Christ.

When Jesus returns, He is looking for a Church without blemish that is producing fruit in accordance with the Scriptures. This bride should be the most powerful group of people on earth because we are betrothed to the most powerful God in the universe. We are made in His image to act and move as He does, doing His will and changing the world for His glory. We cannot do this while we fill ourselves with the pleasures of this world. Our focus should be on purity and preparing ourselves to be servants in His service.

CHAPTER 16

Holy Spirit Power

The Holy Spirit is a powerful force who is part of the Godhead. He was first mentioned in Genesis, accompanying God during creation (Genesis 1:2), signifying He was with God from the beginning. The Godhead or Trinity consists of God the Father, Jesus the Son, and the Holy Spirit. The Trinity is not three different deities but one God existing as three persons. This is a great mystery in which the Spirit of God is an integral part, but few Christians are aware of His importance.

It is imperative to understand the Holy Spirit is a person of the Holy Trinity and is not to be referred to as an *it*. He is sensitive to what we say and do, so care must be taken not to grieve the Holy Spirit. The Holy Spirit is referred to by many names to include the Spirit of God (Genesis 1:2), Spirit of the Lord, Spirit of Wisdom, Spirit of Knowledge, Spirit of Counsel (Isaiah 11:2), Spirit of Grace (Zechariah 12:10), Helper (John 14:16), Spirit of Truth (John 14:17), Comforter (John 14:26), and the Spirit of Life (Romans 8:2) to name a few. These names reflect the broad influence of the Holy Spirit that touches all aspects of the lives of Christians. It is essential we allow the Holy Spirit to move through us so we can fulfill the will of God while benefiting from the power and wisdom His presence brings.

The Holy Spirit is received by a person as a seal of their salvation (Ephesians 1:13). When we choose to follow Jesus, we are accepted by God and have the fullness of His Spirit in us. This fullness accompanies knowledge, wisdom, and power to glorify God. This power is what God wants all believers to walk in, not to satisfy our selfish desires but to do His will and build His kingdom. With the Holy Spirit, we can overcome the devil and live a victorious life.

You may ask, "How can the Holy Spirit help us live a victorious life?" The Holy Spirit has the capacity to give us the gifting needed to be triumphant. These gifts include words of wisdom, words of knowledge, faith, ability to heal, power to do miracles, prophesy, discerning of spirits, speaking in tongues, and the interpretation of a public tongue (1 Corinthians 12:8–10).

Jesus used these gifts while He walked the earth, accomplishing the will of God perfectly. Jesus used wisdom to outwit Satan during His temptation in the wilderness (Matthew 4:1–11), and when the Pharisees questioned His authority, He outmaneuvered them using this gift (Mark 11:28–33). A word of knowledge was used by Jesus in the conversation with the Samaritan woman at the well (John 4:16–18). Even though Jesus had never associated with the woman previously, He was aware of her marital status through divine knowledge. Jesus had unquestionable faith that allowed Him to heal the multitudes (Matthew 15:30–31) and perform uncountable miracles.

By studying these few examples, we can see that the Holy Spirit was an integral part of Jesus's life. Jesus, who was fully God and fully man, gave up His deity and allowed the Holy Spirit to come upon Him in power. Jesus fully admitted His dependence on the Holy Spirit as He spoke the words in Isaiah, "The Spirit of the Lord is upon Me" (Isaiah 61:1). If the Holy Spirit was needed in the earthly ministry of Jesus, how much more important is it for us to have the Holy Spirit as we make disciples? As Jesus modeled how to live in the power of the Holy Spirit, we should adopt this model in our lives. He is the perfect model of how we should function in this current age.

The importance of a relationship with the Holy Spirit was mentioned by Jesus to the apostles before He ascended back into heaven. Jesus instructed the apostles not to leave Jerusalem but to wait for the baptism of the Holy Spirit. Jesus promised the apostles would receive power from the Holy Spirit that would aid them in becoming witnesses for Him (Acts 1:4–8). On the day of Pentecost, the Holy

Spirit indeed did come, filling the house with the sound of a mighty rushing wind, while tongues of fire rested on each of the believers. Instantly, the group was transformed as they spoke in other tongues (Acts 2:2–4). Under the influence of the Holy Spirit, Peter preached a sermon where three thousand people were saved (Acts 2:41), and the apostles performed many wonders and signs (Acts 2:43).

The same Holy Spirit Who allowed the apostles to perform miracles and to speak in tongues is the same Holy Spirit Who worked in Jesus. This proves the Spirit of God can fill people so they can operate in His gifts. If this is the case, why do we not see miracles being performed by Christians today? One reason is many people believe the signs, miracles, and wonders performed by the Holy Spirit through men like the apostles was a onetime event. Since that time period has passed into history, some believe the ability for the Holy Spirit to work through modern believers is also gone.

Nothing could be further from the truth because God does not change. He is looking to work through people who line up with His will and believe in His power. Apostle Paul was not in the upper room but received the Holy Spirit when Ananias prayed for him after his Damascus road experience (Acts 9:17). Under the power of the Holy Spirit, Paul performed several miracles, preached powerful sermons, and wrote several influential letters to the first-century churches. During his ministry, Deacon Stephen, who was full of faith and the power, also did great miracles among the people (Acts 6:8), while Philip the Evangelist performed miracles when preaching to the people in Samaria (Acts 8:4–7). Neither of these individuals were apostles, nor were they mentioned as being in the upper room at Pentecost. Contemporary healers like Smith Wigglesworth and Kathryn Kuhlman displayed the power of the Holy Spirit, performing many miraculous healings witnessed by many people. This is a short list of some of the individuals who allowed the Holy Spirit to flow through them.

Another reason for the absence of Holy Spirit power among believers is a lack of understanding on how to flow in His gifts. This ignorance keeps believers from being sensitive to His promptings and prevents them from responding to His guidance. The Holy Spirit is a gentleman, and He would never force you to do anything you are not comfortable with. Ignoring the Holy Spirit will result in a lack of His presence in your life, thus resulting in a lack of supernatural experiences.

People may not see evidence of the Holy Spirit in their life because they grieve Him by their actions or by living in habitual sin. Scripture warns us we should never be bitter, full of anger, practicing malice, or speaking evil. We should be loving and tender to all mankind, just as God has compassion on us (Ephesians 4:30–32). Humans who live contrary to this godly lifestyle can disturb the Holy Spirit, Who is sensitive to this negative behavior.

Living in sin may also open avenues for demonic spirits to enter into your life. For example, looking at pornography could attract the spirit of lust to attach itself to you. This spirit may be inclined to invite other spirits to come with it, such as the spirit of adultery and fornication. There is no telling how much havoc they could wage in your life. Care should be exercised to refrain from sinning, but when we do, it is important to confess our sins and repent. Allowing sin to go unconfessed and uncleansed by the blood of Jesus is a major obstacle to building a relationship with the Spirit of God.

Not having the infilling of the Holy Spirit in your life can have dire consequences. As stated previously, your body is a temple made for God's Spirit to reside in. If you are not a Christian, the Holy Spirit cannot dwell in you because your sin has not been washed clean by Jesus. If the Holy Spirit is not living in you, this means that your temple is open for other residents. Verses 43 to 45 in Matthew chapter 12 describe this habitation. When a demon leaves a body and finds no other suitable dwelling, it returns to the person from which it came. The demon finds the person has cleaned up their life, but without the protection of the Holy Spirit to fill the temple, there is nothing to stop the demon from invading the body again. This means that demons can take over or possess the body of nonbelievers. Again, the original demon can bring in other evil entities with it, causing more havoc than was experienced before.

Christians cannot be possessed by demons due to the indwelling of the Holy Spirit, but they can be oppressed. This oppression can come in the form of harassment in one's finances, relationships, and day-to-day activities. The only way to squelch the wilds of the demons is to resist them and fully submit to God (James 4:7). By doing this, the demons will flee from your presence. This does not mean the demons will not try to shake your faith, but if you remain submitted to God, the Holy Spirit will be your shield. Jesus was fully submitted to God, and He has full access to the power of the Holy Spirit. This did not stop Satan from trying to tempt and trick Jesus, but the attempts were always foiled by the wisdom and power of God's Spirit.

The Holy Spirit works through men and women who recognize His direction and relinquish control of their lives to Him. Giving up control of one's life can be the hardest thing for most people to do. We want to be the captain of our ship, standing at the wheel and steering to our own destiny. God's Spirit is a much better captain than we will ever be. Allowing the Holy Spirit to use you for God's glory is never usually an easy path, so we must trust Him to direct our lives. Paul suffered beatings, being stoned, shipwrecks, exposure to perils, and other tribulations while serving God. This is not the life most of us would have picked, but the fruit Paul produced through the power of the Holy Spirit supplied us with a large portion of the New Testament. Despite Paul's suffering, he was able to transform the lives of many through his inspiring words as he followed divine guidance, not his own plan.

Further proclamation of the move of the Spirit is outlined in Joel 2:28–29. In these passages, God said He would pour out His Spirit on all flesh to include men and women, both young and old, free and slave. People who acknowledge and allow the Holy Spirit to move through them in boldness and in power will witness the fulfillment of this prophesy. This level of living mandates we do not live in our own flesh but allow God's Spirit to help us supernaturally fight the forces of darkness prevalent in the world today. This is fully iterated in scripture: "Not by might nor by power, but by My Spirit" (Zechariah 4:6)! The qualities of our lives should not be accomplished merely through our own wealth, physical strength, or resources but by our unfailing trust in God. God may use your wealth, strength, and resources to bring Him glory, but this direction should be taken from the Holy Spirit.

Permitting the Spirit of God to guide us and direct our lives ensures we are always in the will of God. This does not mean we sit idly by but work in coordination with the Spirit, following His promptings. He will open up the doors we need to walk through and set up divine meetings when they are needed. All we need to do is pray and then move when the Spirit leads us to move. Following this practice will put you in the right place at the right time.

How do we know when the Spirit is telling us to move? In the Old Testament, the Spirit of God can be seen leading the Israelites through the wilderness as a pillar of cloud during the day and as a column of fire by night (Exodus 13:21). When the Spirit moved, the Israelites packed up their belongings and followed Him. They did not know where they were going or how long they would be traveling, but God's people just followed Him trusting in His guidance. This is how Christians should react to the Holy Spirit. When He moves, we move!

Obviously modern Christians do not have a pillar of clouds or a tower of fire to follow, so we must be sensitive to the quiet voice of the Holy Spirit that calls from within us. This is not usually an audible voice (although sometimes it can be) but comes in the form of thoughts or intuition. This communication can be easily drowned out by the worries and cares of this world. The phrase "be still and know that I am God" (Psalm 46:10) alludes to our spiritual posture as we wait to hear from God. "Be still" does not necessarily relate to lack of activity but refers to quieting your spirit and turning away from all wickedness, anxiety, and other distractions. When you are truly free of worldly pursuits, the Holy Spirit can be heard loud and clear through the spiritual ears of your heart.

Our progress of transitioning from worldly ways to God's format for our existence can be observed in our behavior. The characteristics of the world include sexual immorality, impurity, debauchery, idolatry, hatred, discord, jealousy, rage, selfishness, envy, drunkenness, and orgies (Galatians 5:19–21). These deeds are a good description of the typical way worldly people act today. If the Holy Spirit is in charge of your life, your actions will reflect love, joy, peace, patience, kindness, goodness, faithfulness, gentleness, and self-control (Galatians 5:22–23).

Though no one can fulfill every aspect of the list above perfectly, we should be evaluating our lives to this criterion. There is no other way to achieve the joy and peace people truly desire unless you are filled with the Holy Spirit. Though most Christians do not have all of these characteristics, the Holy Spirit will correct your wrongful actions and place you on the right path of living. All He needs is your obedience to His call and your cooperation so your life will produce the fruits of the Spirit.

Operating in the power of the Holy Spirit is the only true way to live your life. When you "walk in the Spirit, you shall not fulfill the lust of the flesh" (Galatians 5:16). To walk in the Spirit means to follow the Spirit in order to please God, not feeding the desires of the sin nature. The Holy Spirit in us is the best way to resist temptation and stay free from the snares of the evil one. Satan cannot win against the Holy Spirit Who lives in you because greater is He (Holy Spirit) who lives in me than he (devil) who lives in the world (1 John 4:4). If you try to fight the devil in your own strength, he will win every time.

You are not stronger than Satan, but God is! So we have to be diligent to the calling of the Spirit of God. Without Him, we become easy prey for the devil. With Him, we dwell in safety, free from the deception of Satan. So in all things, pray and sit in quiet meditation on the Word of God, listening as wisdom is given to you. Christians should always be living their lives in a godly manner by being bridled to the Holy Spirit. With the Holy Spirit on our side, we are always victorious. Besides, when we reach our final destination, we want to hear, "Well done good and faithful servant."

CHAPTER 17

The Power of the Blood

Everyone at one time or another has probably heard the Bible verse from John 3:16: "God so loved the world that He gave His only begotten Son, so that whoever believes in Him shall not perish, but have everlasting life." If you have accepted the Lord Jesus Christ as your Savior, you understand the importance of this verse and the need for His cleansing blood. If you are not a Christian, you may be confused about the references in this book proclaiming His saving grace. In this chapter, we will examine this redeeming power and explain why His dying on the cross was necessary.

In the beginning, we know the Garden of Eden was the residence of Adam and Eve. God made the garden for mankind, and His perfect plan would have been for us to live out our days in the peace and abundance He provided. God, being omniscient (all-knowing), knew that man would rebel against Him and eat from the forbidden tree, condemning future generations with the sin nature that leads to destruction. In His goodness, He devised a plan to redeem the future of mankind from an eternity in hell to a life forever in heaven with Him. This plan is John 3:16.

When Jesus was born into this world, He was born a man but was fully God. Jesus was fully God because Mary was impregnated by the Holy Spirit, a deposit of God's seed, making God the Father of Jesus. Jesus was born through a woman, making Him fully man because He was born in the flesh. Jesus being fully God did not use the powers of His deity but lived life as we do feeling pain, temptation, and suffering. The only difference is Jesus lived His life perfectly without committing any sin. Sin was brought into this world by one man's disobedience (Adam) and was passed down as an inheritance to all mankind. Just as one act of disobedience ushered sin into this world, another man's obedient life washes it away. Jesus conquered sin by being compliant to God's commandments, and He wants to trade His perfect, sinless life for your imperfect, sinful existence.

So why did Jesus have to die in order for us to be free from sin? In biblical days, if a Hebrew sinned, they would bring a bull, goat, or lamb to the Jewish temple and present it to the priest. The sinner would then lay their hand upon the head of the animal, a representation of the transference of sin from the human to the beast. Since the wages of sin is death (Romans 6:23), a life had to be taken, and the animal was the substitute for the human. The killing of the animal paid the price for the transgression of the sinner fulfilling their debt. This was a precursor of the sacrifice of Jesus on the cross, an act that completely exonerated our sin. Jesus died and shed His blood to become a substitute for us so we could be set free from the punishment of sin. When you accept Jesus as your Lord and Savior, He gives you this privilege as a free gift.

You may wonder how you trade your life of sin for the perfect life of Jesus. Touching the head of an animal is tangible, but you cannot physically touch Jesus. The Bible states, "If you declare with your mouth that Jesus is Lord and believe in your heart that God raised Him from the dead, you will be saved" (Romans 10:9). To believe in your heart means to be convinced beyond a shadow of a doubt Jesus lived a perfect life, died shedding His blood as payment for your sins, and was then resurrected. This is just not an idea in your mind but a strong conviction every fiber of your being knows to be true.

When you confess this belief with your mouth, you have made a public announcement of your confidence that the love of God has redeemed you. This process propagates a total lifestyle change that directs you away from sin and connects you to living a godly existence. A true conversion is an event you will remember for the rest of your life because of its profound impact. Just like you would not forget your birthday or the day you got married, you will never forget the day you were saved.

There still is another important component to God's plan. With the animal sacrifices, every time a person sinned, another animal would have to be killed. This was part of the old covenant way for atonement, but the blood of animals could not take away sins (Hebrews 10:4). The practice was foreshadowing the sacrifice of the Lamb of God, the Lord Jesus Christ. Sin is a spiritual problem that cannot be eliminated with a physical act but needs a spiritual solution. When Jesus shed His blood for us on the cross, His sacrifice is the spiritual fix that forgives all of our sins—past, present, and future. Sin is dead in us when we live in Christ.

Many people who go to church are deceived about their salvation, believing they are heaven bound when they may be going to hell. Most churches profess that saying a simple prayer will guarantee you a spot in heaven. Without a heart change and solid belief in the sacrifice of Jesus, this prayer is nothing but an empty promise. It is with your heart that you believe unto righteousness (Romans 10:10), not just with the speaking of words. The evidence of a false conversation can be witnessed when the life of the alleged convert remains unchanged over time.

True conversions produce fruit in alignment with the character of God. If nothing is changing in your life, there is a need to closely examine your relationship with God. A life lived for God is a life that does not actively pursue sin. Those who confess to be saved (converted believers of Jesus) but practice the wickedness of the world have not experienced the grace of God. To love God is to hate sin. Do not allow yourself to be deceived. It is a trap of Satan.

Some people who are converted may have a Damascus road experience like Paul and be instantly on fire for God. Most of us, however, will experience a gradual change in our lifestyle as we grow in Christ. We may try to continue in the conduct of the life we lived before our conversion, but the Holy Spirit will convict us of our sin. When we do something ungodly, this conviction will be a stirring of our spirit that produces a feeling we perceive as correction. This conviction may not be strong at first, but it will be constant. The strength of the conviction grows as our relationship with Christ matures. You may continue to sin for a period of time, but the consistent prompting of the Holy Spirit will cause the true Christian to turn away or repent from their sin. Some sins may drop away quickly; others may remain for a time, but sin will eventually be mastered through maturity in Christ Jesus. This does not mean we will never stumble and sin again, but our resistance to sin will be greatly enhanced.

To the unbeliever who has not experienced salvation, the conversion may seem like a difficult and confusing transition. If you have been living your life without God, changing your lifestyle may not make a lot of sense to you. Your mind has been conditioned to accept your current routine as the only way to live. Only by renewing your mind can you truly see things as God sees them.

When Ananias prayed for Paul (Acts 9: 10–18), the scriptures state, "Something like scales" fell from his eyes, and he regained his sight. I believe this passage in part is referring to the revelation Paul received from the Holy Spirit as Ananias prayed. Paul now had a different perspective and obtained knowledge of life through the eyes of Christ.

Praying to God to send His Holy Spirit to give you this revelation is a great way to get this insight. If you are not sure how to pray, ask a believer to pray with you for your salvation. God knows when a person is asking with a sincere heart. The devil will probably fill your mind with all kinds of foolishness during the prayer to convince you that what you are doing is stupid—thoughts like, *What will your family and friends think of you if they knew what you were doing?* Or *Look at all the fun stuff you will have to give up if you become a Christian?* Once the Holy Spirit gives you an appreciation of how much God loves you and that He was willing to put His Son on the cross for your sins, you can overcome those doubts. Once you are saved, you will wonder why you waited so long. It is really not that difficult.

It is important for new Christians to realize salvation is a gift from God you cannot earn. Many Christians will try to justify their newfound faith by doing good deeds. Paul said salvation is "not by works, so that no one can boast" (Ephesians 2:9). We do good works because we love God, and we want to glorify Him. These are actions we perform in humility, bringing the focus onto God and not on ourselves. If you are bragging about the ministry you are doing, this is a form of pride that does not honor God but puts the attention on you. If the duties you are doing are only glorifying you and not God, then you need to examine your underlying intentions. Besides, no one is good enough to work their way into heaven. Jesus is the only man who lived a sinless life.

If the Holy Spirit is prompting you to accept Jesus, you can speak from your heart and surrender your life to Him. If you do not have the words to say, you can say the words below. Remember, it is not the words that are important but that you are confessing them from your heart.

> Lord Jesus, I know that I am a sinner and that You died for my sins. I want You to be the Lord of my life, and I am willing to give myself to You. I believe You died on the cross and that God raised You from the dead. I believe Your sacrifice will atone for all my sins, so I repent (turn away) of my transgressions and turn toward Your commandments as a way to live my life. When I sin again, I will confess my sins to You, repent, and ask for Your forgiveness. Jesus, thank You for saving me. Amen.

If you just prayed a prayer for your salvation with all your heart, welcome to the family of God. A word of caution: the devil will try to steal this seed of salvation away from you and cast doubt on the decision you have just made. It is important to get involved in a local church as soon as possible and find mature Christians who are willing to disciple you and help you on your journey. Get to know God by studying the Bible while always keeping the lines of communication open with Him through prayer. As with any relationship, this new life may seem awkward at first, but as you grow in Christ, it will be your new normal.

Exercise sober judgment as you start your Christian walk. Your enemy, Satan, will be trying his best to wreak havoc in every part of your life. Now that you have a relationship with God and carry His Holy Spirit, you are a real threat to him. The devil will do everything he can to make you doubt your salvation and discourage your work in Christ. Sharpen your ability to listen to the Holy Spirit and be comforted that you are not alone. Surround yourself with other Christians who can support you as you grow in your faith. Study and learn all you can about the nature of God, the building blocks to a stronger relationship with Him. When things get tough (and they will), remember, the God of the universe is on your side.

CHAPTER 18

Death Is Not the End

Most people fear death because as humans, we tend to be afraid of the unknown. There are books and movies where people claimed to have died and experienced the afterlife, but many have doubts on whether these claims are true or just hallucinations produced during the dying process. There are many unanswered questions when it comes to death, leaving people with apprehension by just mentioning the subject. If you are a Christian, you need not fear death because Jesus has overcome death and the grave. As discussed, His death on the cross paid for our sins so we can have eternal life.

Proof of Jesus's power over death can be observed in several Bible passages. For example, the resurrection power of God can be witnessed in the story of Lazarus of Bethany, the brother of Martha and Mary (John 11). Jesus arrived at the home of Lazarus after he had been dead for several days. The confirmation of Lazarus's death was validated by the smell of his decomposing corpse.

Upon His arrival, Jesus was confronted by Martha, expressing her wish that He would have visited sooner so her brother would not have died. Martha's understanding seemed to suggest the power of God could only operate when a person was still living, but Jesus responded to her by saying, "I am the resurrection and the life" (John 11:25). Though Martha agreed with Jesus, I do not believe she fully comprehended the depth of this statement until Lazarus was called out of the tomb totally restored. Indeed, many of the Jews mourning with Martha and Mary that day believed in Jesus after they observed this astonishing miracle.

Jesus did not perform this miracle in secret but in the presence of many people. In the Scriptures, it states after Jesus heard Lazarus was sick, He still waited two days to visit him. Jesus did this on purpose, knowing Lazarus would be dead, so He could display His power over death. Jesus was not so much concerned with the physical death of Lazarus because He was the keeper of his soul, and in Him, Lazarus lived (spiritually). The devil may take our physical bodies, but he cannot consume a person's spirit if they are in Christ. Jesus's power over death was proven by raising Lazarus and others from the dead. The flesh will eventually expire and decay, an experience that seems very sad to most people but is not important in the grand scheme of eternity. The most important decision should be made for the preservation of the soul. Those who do not chose Jesus as Lord will be tormented by Satan in the eternal flames. The devil desires your soul, not your body, and if the devil succeeds in procuring your soul, this will truly be a sad day for the person who is lost.

Further proof of the power of God over death is illustrated by the crucifixion of Jesus and His resurrection. Jesus was not crucified in secret but in a public display, where many people could attest to His death. Jesus's death was also confirmed by a Roman soldier, who pierced His side with a spear as blood and water rushed out of His body (John 19:34). When Jesus rose from the grave, He appeared to several people before He ascended into heaven. Jesus did this miracle in public so all who witnessed these events could testify to the truth and believe.

Physical death of the body is only a transition or doorway into the supernatural realm. As an ugly caterpillar is evolved into a beautiful butterfly, death is the change from this life to the next. When Satan told Eve before she ate the forbidden fruit that "you will not surely die" (Genesis 3:4), he was deceiving her. At first, it appears Satan was truthful because Adam and Eve did not die instantly after consuming the fruit. Their eternal status was revoked, however, and their physical presence on earth would not last forever but would be limited as humans are today. When the physical life has ended, those who did not accept Jesus as their Savior will be condemned to hell for eternity. For those who trust in Jesus, however, the doorway opens to an afterlife that includes God, with a joy and peace that accompanies His Spirit. Believers will be given a glorious new body (Philippians 3:21), and Jesus will give us a new name better suited for our character (Revelation 2:17). As scary as our physical death seems, for those who believe in Christ, it leads to an existence we cannot mentally conceive while we are alive.

When it comes to death, there are many different options. Some people believe there is no afterlife, while others believe there is no hell. The Bible states although your body will one day cease to function, your spirit will continue to live eternally. The residence of your spirit will be one of two places: heaven or hell. Proof of this statement is illustrated in the story about the rich man and the beggar Lazarus. The rich man who lived a lavish life and refused to show pity on Lazarus experienced torment in hell after his death. On the other side of the spectrum, Lazarus's final residence was heaven (Luke 16:22–25). These passages clearly state there is a paradise and a place of torment in the afterlife. The rich man was self-absorbed and had no compassion for his neighbor, who was obviously in need. His reward due to his lack of love for his brethren was the place of anguish, while Lazarus rested in bliss.

Matthew 25 further illuminates the concept of heaven and hell. In verse 34, the King (Jesus) called to the righteous, who had compassion on their fellow man, to come enjoy the kingdom (heaven) prepared for them since the beginning of time. The wicked ones, who did not help their brothers in need, were cursed to the eternal fire (hell) made for the devil and his demons (verse 41). The parable outlines those who serve others were performing a service for the King, and their reward is the eternal kingdom of heaven, while the wicked servants, who were self-serving, face eternal punishment. This does not mean you earn a place in heaven through good works, but people who believe in Jesus have the same character and demonstrate this disposition by serving others. Those who do not abide in Christ are usually self-serving and carnal in nature, and their actions reflect this type of personality.

Matthew 25 also illustrates an important point that hell was not made for man but for the devil and his demons. God's wish is for nobody to go to hell, however, if you do not accept the free gift of salvation, you will receive a demon's reward. The good news is while you are still breathing, it is never too late to accept Jesus.

The book of Revelation contains information about heaven and hell as being two very real places. Apostle John describes heaven when he was taken up in the Spirit to the throne room of God. John saw a rainbow around the throne of God that was glorious in color, while lightning and thunder filled the background. Strange creatures surrounded the throne, and their main job was to worship the Lord God (Revelation 4). If anything, heaven does not sound like a boring place where believers will be floating on a cloud playing a harp but a place filled with action and excitement. The grandeur of heaven experienced by John probably could not be fully expressed with his words, nor could they capture the intensity of the sounds and emotions associated with being in the presence of God.

John also talks about a new heaven and earth that will be created after the first heaven and earth pass away. He also describes a New Jerusalem descending from the heavens as being spectacular and appearing as a bride adorned for her husband (Revelation 21:2). The city walls are lined with precious stones, and the gates are made from a single large pearl. The New Jerusalem is described as containing the glory of God, which illuminates the city so the sun is not needed. Flowing from the throne of God is the river of life that supplies water to the tree of life, a plant that bears fruit for every season and has healing properties in its leaves for the nations (Revelation 21–22).

Hell, on the other hand, is described as a lake of fire filled with brimstone, where the residents will be tormented day and night forever and ever (Revelation 14:10–11). Have you ever been burned by a flame? The pain associated with a burn is excruciating to say the least. Can you image feeling the pain of being surrounded by flames scorching your entire body for an eternity? This is an awful situation to think about, but you do not have to experience this pain because God has given you a lifeboat, and His name is Jesus.

With that being said, most people still worry about the physical death of the body more than they worry about spiritual separation from God. For people who have not heard about Jesus, this is to be an expected reaction to passing away. If this life is all you have, the end would result with great sorrow. This is why Jesus wants His faithful ones to tell all people about His plan so unbelievers will have the opportunity to live for Him.

There are also those individuals who know about Jesus but choose the ways of the world. This is a critical error, for they are trading their souls for something that is only temporary. While they are still alive, it is the job of Christians to inform them about the foolishness of their choice. Believers may not be able to convince them to change their minds, but these people will at least be exposed to the truth.

Even some Christians worry about the end of their lives. The devil will always try to fill your mind with doubt, but anxiety about death may be an indication your trust in Jesus needs to be strengthened. Build your relationship with Him by spending more time in His embrace. Praying, reading God's Word, and worship are always a good starting point. Relationships are always strengthened when your heart comes into alignment with the heart of the King.

Do not fear death and the unknown but trust in God to deliver you from the evil of this world. Sin is the cause of decay in this world, and in heaven, there will be no such problem because there will be no sin. For those who believe in Jesus, their worst times will exist in this world. The afterlife will be a condition of sheer peace and joy, for all believers will be in the presence of God Himself.

CHAPTER 19

Community

It is written where two or three gather together in His name, He will be among them (Matthew 18:20). This concept can first be observed in the book of Genesis, where God visited Adam and Eve in the cool of the day (Genesis 3:8). God created man so He could form a bond of fellowship with people who willingly choose to love Him. If you have not realized it yet, God is all about relationships. Since we are made in His image, we are designed to be connected to God and to one another. If we join together as one body of believers under the guidance of the Holy Spirit, nothing will be impossible for us.

God's plan is not to have just a small group of people who believe in Him but for the Church to grow and expand to include as many believers as possible. The purpose of Jesus's disciplining the apostles was not for them to keep the good news to themselves but to spread the Word to as many people as possible. Modern-day believers in the Lord Jesus Christ have this same mission. Any group of people who can move as a continuous and fluid body can powerfully influence the culture, and this is exactly what the Church is designed to do. We are to be world changers, united as one under God. The devil despises the thought of the Church being on one page, and he does not want that plan to flourish. If the Church of the Lord God became of one accord, the days of Satan would surely be numbered.

In order to stop the progression of the Church, the devil uses his old tactics of divide and conquer. For example, the Christian

Church is divided up into many different denominations, each having a slightly different interpretation of Scripture and understanding of how to live the Christian life. The different principles and interpretations fracture the Church into many facets. If believers could all agree on the important doctrine that Jesus died to save us from hell and God raised Him from the dead, the unity would promote a revival of biblical proportions in the modern-day Church. It is not religious rules and regulations that build the body of Christ; it is the love for God and others that develops community.

As we honor God's commandment to love our neighbors as ourselves, a corporate anointing is manifested upon the community. This is the type of anointing experienced by the apostles at Pentecost, a harmony that attracted the Holy Spirit, who immediately filled them with His presence. When people come together with one heart and one mind bound with love, these members become an unstoppable power against the forces of evil. This becomes apparent after the visit of the Holy Spirit at Pentecost. With Holy Spirit power, the apostles were praising God in other tongues as the crowds of different nationalities listened in amazement. Peter stepped in and preached a sermon that resulted in three thousand members being added to the Church. Under the corporate anointing, miracles became commonplace, while love poured out of the hearts of believers to support those in need (Acts 2). This is the representation of what the true Church should be like.

This sense of community is the power of God where the focus is not on one person but on the entire population working as one. Self-centeredness is the enemy of community, and there is no room for that mentality in the Church. A lot of modern-day churches preach about how to receive the blessing of God rather than blessing God. When the focus is on God and operating in His will, the blessings come to you automatically. When going to church becomes all about how you can profit from it, you are putting yourself as the focal point. The behavior of just looking out for number one leaves no room for caring about others or loving God—thus, you are outside of the will of God. Humble yourself and cast your eyes upon the

Creator as you love His people, then you will know true blessings and joy unspeakable.

God wants to build a community of followers who will encourage each other so anyone will be strengthened. No one should try to live the Christian life alone since working as a group is far easier than going about it individually. If you try serving Jesus on your own, then you will be an easy target for the devil. In nature, predators separate a member of the herd in order to wear down their prey so they can ultimately destroy them. Satan uses the same strategy in an attempt to separate you from other believers so he can weaken your faith and undermine your trust in God. If the devil can disconnect you from the Truth and fill your head with lies, he can use this leverage for your destruction.

In the parable of the Lost Sheep (Matthew 18:12), the shepherd left the ninety-nine to chase after the one that was lost. I believe the shepherd did this knowing there is safety in numbers, but the lost sheep that was separated from the flock was more vulnerable. Do not be a lone ranger. There is security in numbers. Get involved in a Bible-believing, God-fearing church, where you can grow and better learn how to serve God.

As Christians, we are part of something bigger than ourselves, and we all have a special purpose to serve. Apostle Paul, in his letter to the Corinthians, talks about this very subject. He states the body is made up of many members, each having a different function (1 Corinthians 12:12–31). No part of the body can operate without the rest of the body, and no one part is more important than the other. Paul goes on to say that God made the parts of the body diverse so it can perform more effectively. If the body only had a head, then what would accomplish the job of the hands, feet, and so forth?

In the body of Christ, God made some to be apostles, prophets, evangelists, pastors, and teachers for the equipping of the saints to perform God's will (Ephesians 4:11–12). If everyone was a prophet, who would teach and interpret the prophecies that were spoken? If there were no evangelists, who would reach converts and spread the Word of God? If there were no pastors, then who would lead the church and care for the people? Too many of the same components in the body creates an imbalance. God made us different for a good reason, so never discount your talents when you are using them to serve the Lord. He has made you perfectly with the ability to serve Him while completing the body as a whole. Just as you would not want to lose even your pinky finger, God made every part of the Church to be essential and useful for His good works.

There are many other reasons why fellowship among Christians is vital. The nurturing of the saints can only be accomplished through relationships. All Christians are at different levels of development, and we all need help in our walk with God. Some believers have walked with the Lord for a long period of time, experiencing His goodness as He has worked in their lives. This wealth of knowledge can be shared with new converts who have yet to encounter the guiding hand of the Holy Spirit. Christians who have overcome the snares of the devil dealing with problems such as addictions, broken marriages, and sickness can give direction to those who are currently going through a similar trial. Those who are being beaten down by an attack of Satan can be lifted up with encouragement by others who have weathered the storm. No one person knows it all, and we need each other's support, edification, and revelation to grow in Christ. There is a lot of truth in the proverb "as iron sharpens iron, so one man sharpens another" (Proverbs 27:17).

Accountability is also a large part of community. If left to our own devises while exposed to the influences of this world's culture, we will most likely fall into a trap prepared for us by the devil. Communing with other believers will strengthen you and keep you from making bad decisions inspired by the flesh. The values of the world should not be shaping the Church; the Church should be reforming the moral climate of the world. This can only be accomplished by changing one person at a time until the Word of God has permeated their hearts.

In order to change the standards of the flesh, Christians must have a strong resolve. Having a Christian friend you can confide in can help you stay on the straight and narrow as you develop a stellar character. You can talk to this person about your weaknesses and how the devil may be tempting you to sin. This confidant may be able to counsel you through the use of scripture or pray with you for strength and revelation on how to solve your dilemma. It is always easier to go through a problem when you have someone to share the pain with.

A word of caution: the devil will do anything in his power to stop you from sharing your pain with others because accountability is only beneficial if you truthfully confess your issues to another person. The devil will usually use shame and guilt to cause embarrassment so you will not discuss the situation with other believers. By doing so, he will successfully keep a hold on you. By confessing our weakness to others, the powers of darkness are dissipated by the truth spoken to us through love. Having a trusted accountability partner is a great way to overcome the bondages of the enemy and experience true freedom.

Meeting the needs of others is an important part of community. People in need who are not connected to others can feel isolated, thinking there is no solution to their problem. Being a helping hand was an integral part of the early Christian Church. When the Greek widows were not receiving their food allowance, a group of seven men were chosen to ensure the necessities of all the women were met (Acts 6:1–3). These deacons who served these women provided a great benefit, bringing hope to a hopeless situation. In this day, there are a lot of people searching for hope in a callous, cruel world, and you can be the person who introduces them to that hope, the Lord Jesus.

Jesus said in the last days, lawlessness would be prevalent, and the hearts of men would grow cold (Matthew 24:12). It appears this prophesy is in the works in this current age. Who knows how much worse the ethical attitude of humanity will get as time marches forth. The only practical way to endure this brutal exposure is in the safety of community, with fellow believers united to care for one another and reach the world.

CHAPTER 20

Power of the Tongue

The tongue is a small part of the body, and you probably do not give it a lot of thought. Although the tongue is not great in size, the power it possesses can be potent. The Bible says life and death are in the power of the tongue (Proverbs 18:21). We can speak from the goodness of God's perspective (life) or a negative posture devised from evil (death). We are free to choose to speak either life or death, but we must live with the consequences of our decision. Have you ever said something ugly to someone and instantly regretted it? Once inappropriate verbiage leaves your mouth, there is no getting it back. When we fail to rein in our tongue, the damage we can cause in a few seconds can alter the course of our lives. In a sudden outburst, you can speak out vulgarities in a fit of rage, severing relationships and destroying associations that took years to build. How can something seemingly so minute have the ability to cause so much damage?

In the book of James, the author compares the tongue to a small rudder that steers the course of a massive ship or a bit that controls the actions of a powerful stallion (James 3:3–4). These are strong comparisons demonstrating how much authority this member commands. This is why it is always important to think before you speak. James goes on to describe the potential of a loose tongue as "an unruly evil, full of deadly poison" (verse 8). Although the words we speak can be damaging, it is not what God designed our tongues to do. He created the tongue to praise Him and to speak blessings.

This tool of praise and blessing can be used as an instrument of destruction if one is under the control of the sin nature. Only those who operate in the Spirit of Christ Jesus can use the tongue for the purpose it was truly meant for.

The power of the tongue is first illuminated during creation in the book of Genesis. Here we can learn how God spoke into existence the heavens and the earth. This is the kind of capability the spoken word can have. You may be thinking, *My words cannot possibly have that much potential. Besides, He can create anything with a word because He is God.* As true as this is, we must remember we are made in the image of God and possess His qualities. I am not saying you will speak worlds and planets into existence, but you have more power in the spoken word than you realize. Have you ever made the statement, "I think I am getting a headache," and within a short period of time, you find you are experiencing exactly what you have spoken of? Your subconscious mind is a great servant, and it is always looking to fulfill your request. If it is a headache you want, the subconscious mind can surely accommodate you. Speak positive words and blessings into your life and the subconscious mind will be programmed to search out and recognize opportunities to suit your guest. Never underestimate God's design of your mind to act as you command it to respond.

This is why it is important to renew your mind (Romans 12:2) so you think the same way God thinks and not as the world does. What you believe about yourself will be spoken through your tongue. You should only speak godly beliefs about yourself such as you are perfectly and wonderfully made for God's purpose, or you are an overcomer.

People with low self-esteem often speak negative things about themselves such as, "I am not smart," or "I am not a good person." The truth may be you have a greater capacity to learn than most people, but by saying you are stupid, the bar for improvement is set low. This type of attitude stifles your desire to increase your knowledge by studying, a practice that will expand your intelligence and build your confidence. If you keep repeating phrases like you are not a good person, this will alter how you feel about yourself and how you approach people. What you speak over yourself is powerful and will direct the path of your life.

Great care must be taken when you talk to other people, especially children. Children, unlike adults, do not have a filter to sort out the destructive criticism from constructive advice. Any hurtful word coming out of the mouth of an authority figure in a child's life will be taken as the truth. If you tell your child repeatedly that they are stupid, do not be surprised if they do not do well in school.

Derogatory words spoken to adults can also provoke disparaging results. Harsh words may reinforce negative beliefs a person has about themselves, fueling internal turmoil, further lowering their self-esteem. Some people may take your criticism as an insult and react in a retaliatory manner. Whatever the case, negative words usually generate an unfavorable response, so take extra caution of how you speak to others.

The use of one's tongue can divulge a lot about a person's character. Telling lies in this modern day has become so commonplace, many people do not think twice about it. Regularly lying in politics, business transactions, and in relationships has become an accepted custom considered necessary to get ahead. Today's culture would say there is no harm in telling a little white lie or stretching the truth a bit. Jesus would disagree with this philosophy because He delights in those who tell the truth and refrain from lying. He condemned those who continually lied as being sons of the devil, who is the father of lies (John 8:44). Lying may seem like a quick way to get what you want, but lying just gets you into bondage. When you stack lie upon lie, it becomes hard to remember the last lie you fabricated. Sooner or later, a person who habitually lies will be discovered as one who lacks integrity. Their reputation will be damaged, and the trust others placed in them will quickly diminish.

Flattery is another tool used to manipulate others to achieve a selfish agenda. Any time you use flattery to manipulate people for your gain, you are practicing a form of deception. Deception is something God does not approve of, and we are warned to be wary of those who use smooth words and flattering speech (Romans 16:18). We are to love our neighbor, not use them as a means to an end.

Similar to lying, flattery is a characteristic of the devil, who disguises himself as an angel of light to deceive the unknowing. Learn to tame your tongue so you do not fall into the habit of charming others for your gain.

Gossip is a pastime people love to participate in. Standing around the water fountain at work, employees love to talk about the boss and other coworkers. God warns us to let no corrupting talk come out of our mouths but to only use language that edifies others (Ephesians 4:29). If you are talking bad about someone behind their back, you are tearing them down. One of the dangers with gossip is it may get back to the person you are talking about. Not only will this cause you great embarrassment, but it could potentially result in damage to the relationship. In addition, always remember the people who are gossiping with you may be the same ones who are gossiping about you when you are not there. Think about this the next time you get the urge to gossip about someone else.

Cursing is the act of speaking evil and misfortune over some-one's circumstances. This is a purely demonic activity and should not be performed by God's people. Think back to a time in your life when you got angry and responded with the phrase like, "I wish you were dead." This is a curse. Of course, you may have not meant it, but you must remember the power your words carry.

God wants us to speak blessings over people and refrain from cursing them (Romans 12:14). Even when people hurt you very badly, Christians are expected to love their enemies and not repay evil for evil (Romans 12:17). Take an example from Jesus. Even when He was being severely beaten and mocked during His crucifixion, no unkind word came from His lips. When the criminals who were being executed with Jesus verbally attacked Him, He only spoke life to the one who requested His blessing. We are to be like Jesus, ones who are called to love and bless all people no matter how they treat us. This can be a difficult order, but God will give you the strength to endure persecution if you follow His commands.

Lying, flattery, gossip, and cursing are just a few of the ways the tongue can be used to perpetuate evil. The tongue, if used correctly, however, can be a pathway to blessing and peace. Most people have some type of anxiety and stress in their life, but the fashion in which you address the problem determines what the outcome will be. A lot of people tend to focus on their issues and verbally express them by complaining, an exercise that embellishes the difficulty, not the solution. Focusing on the irritations only increases the anxiety, allowing it to take further hold in your life. If you use your tongue to pray and hand your trials over to God, then the Bible promises that great peace will be your portion (Philippians 4:6–7). God's yoke is easy, and His burden is light (Matthew 11:30), so why try to carry the burden by yourself? When you have God on your team, He will help you and support the brunt of the load.

Using your tongue to pray can also be an entranceway into the realm of the supernatural. If you study the life of Jesus, you will see He spent a considerable amount of time praying. His prayer life revolved around finding out the will of Father God and then proceeding to carry out those directives. Jesus used the spoken word to command out demons, cure sickness, and raise the dead. The words Jesus used to perform these miracles were blessed by God and acted upon by the Holy Spirit to produce a supernatural result. Jesus spoke words of truth and blessing, the same words He heard the Father speaking. If we pray and seek out God's will, He will bless the words we speak, and the Holy Spirit will respond to our request. I have seen people healed by prayer and others delivered from demonic bondages with a simple command. It is important to remember God's Holy Spirit is the power behind the supernatural, and He will use this power to assist us when we act on behalf of God's good purpose.

One of the most important functions of the tongue is to praise God. When we praise God, we put everything into perspective. We acknowledge He is God, and we are not. When responding to the call of God, it is important to come before Him with an attitude of gratitude and praise. This is the mechanism that ignites thankfulness and initiates humility in a person. I believe it is one of the reasons why praise is made for us. God is not trying to get us to glorify Him because He is an egomaniac who feeds on affirmation. God is trying to position us in the right posture so we will be ready to respond to His call.

When we hold back praise from God, we are acting like the devil. Satan's pride drove him to withhold praise from God and seek praise for himself. This mentality led to his fall from grace, and the same will happen to you if you follow this path. Use the tongue for what it is made for, to praise God, then watch your life begin to flourish. Praising God is truly the way to open the windows of heaven.

Worship can come in many forms, but verbal worship by singing songs and hymns can be a powerful medium to connect to God. Corporate worship services in a church or Christian gathering can multiply the anointing and be an invitation for the manifest presence of God. A lot of people refuse to sing in front of others, fearing their ability to sing will be judged substandard. Even if their vocal quality was poor, most could become better if they would just open their mouths. Even if you were the worst vocalist ever, God will still cherish your worship. Like a parent who watches their young child at a recital with pride, though the performance may not be spectacular, how much more would God beam over you. Never miss an opportunity to worship God no matter how tone-deaf you may think you are.

One of the most important uses of the tongue is telling others about Jesus. One of the acts we should be doing while we are alive on this planet is making disciples of all nations (Matthew 28:19). God wants us to spread the gospel to the far ends of the earth so everyone will have the chance to hear it and believe. Talking to people about the good news of Jesus is the best gift you can give them. Do not be afraid of what other people will think but take comfort you are performing God's work and snatching souls from the grasp of hell.

God created your tongue so you could speak words of life and blessing, so use it to praise and worship Him while you tell others about His grace. As you change the way you think and speak, your life will begin to change for the better. Jesus used His tongue to change the world, and if you are ready, He will use you to do the same.

CHAPTER 21

He Is Coming Back

There is a story about a man who left to go on a long journey to a foreign land, but before leaving, he entrusted his belongs to his servant's care. Each servant was given a different percentage of the estate to manage according to their ability. Those who were more capable were given much and smaller portions were given to those who had less proficiency, but all were given something to oversee. Those who were wise used the master's riches to receive a return on their investment. Some, however, did not use their competence to increase the worth of their master's estate and its value remained unchanged. After a long time, the noble man returned home and gathered his servants to evaluate their progress. Those who invested wisely were lavished with the master's praise and were rewarded. The servants who did nothing to generate a profit were rebuked and forsaken by the master (Matthew 25:14–29).

The dialogue above is a parable told by Jesus about His return, with the master of course being a metaphor representing the Lord Jesus Christ. That's right, Jesus is coming back and when He does, He will be looking for His faithful servants. The faithful servants are Christians who have been entrusted with using their God-given talents to enlarge the body of Christ. It is a believer's duty to tell others about the kingdom of heaven (God's estate) and Jesus's sacrifice for our salvation. Making new converts and disciplining them in the ways of Christ should be a top priority for Christians. People who keep quiet and do nothing to promote the free gift of Jesus are like the servants who did nothing to benefit their Master, refusing to use their own ability to build the kingdom. Like the noble man in the story above, Jesus blesses those He finds doing His business.

Many people today scoff at the idea Jesus will return someday and reject the concept like it was some sort of fairy tale. The servants of the noble man probably thought the same thing about their master after he was gone for a very long time. It is easy to become complacent since Jesus's return has also been a long time in coming, but what a sad day it will be for those who are caught not taking care of His affairs when He does return. The Bible says Jesus will descend from heaven and all His faithful ones will be caught up in the clouds to meet Him (1 Thessalonians 4:16–17). This will be a glorious day for those who believe in Jesus, for they will have a permanent residence in the kingdom of heaven. Nobody but God knows when this day will be, but the Bible warns us several times how important it is we are not caught unprepared. Being prepared means accepting Jesus as your Lord and Savior, then living your life in a manner that brings God glory.

The end-time visit of the Lord Jesus happens in two events, the rapture and the second coming. The Thessalonians 4 scripture mentioned above is referring to the rapture of the Church. For those who are not familiar with this term, the rapture is where the dead in Christ will rise from their graves and living Christians will physically leave this earth to be joined with God. Only true believers will see Jesus and be called up into the clouds to join Him. During this transition, we will be given glorified bodies and will be rewarded by God for the work we have done in His name. The world will probably be at a loss to explain the mass disappearance of so many people at one time, while confusion and chaos will likely erupt as people frantically search for answers.

The rapture and the second coming of Christ revolve around the Tribulation Period, a seven-year timeframe marking the end of the age. At first glance, the start of the Tribulation will appear to be a renaissance of a new world order filled with unity and peace ushered in by a charismatic world leader. During the first three and a half years, the new ruler will gain increasing prestige by solving many problems and resolving conflicts in the world. After the half way point is reached, however, the leader will take on a new light proclaiming to be God. This person, who is the antichrist (one possessed by Satan), will demand a one world religion which worships and pays allegiance to only him. Those who refuse to bow down to the antichrist will be executed as a warning to others who may be thinking about not complying with the edict. All people who submit to this decree will be forced to take on the symbol of their new master referred to as the Mark of the Beast (Revelation 13:16–17). This identifier will allow only those who have it the privilege to operate in the market place. All others who do not possess the mark will be unable to buy the most basic daily necessities. This will all be orchestrated under a one world government where the antichrist dominates all nations with an iron rule.

Although the exact day of the rapture is only known by God, many have speculated the point during the Tribulation in which this event will take place. The timing of the rapture has several different hypotheses, but they all fall into three basic categories. Some believe since we are God's children, Christians will not be exposed to the wrath of the Tribulation, but that believers will be raptured before it starts. Other parties theorize the rapture will take place in the middle of the Tribulation before things really start to get ugly, sparing us the pain associated with the last three and a half years referred to as the Great Tribulation. The less popular idea is Christians will have to persevere through some or all of the Tribulation and Christ will return just before or during the second coming to retrieve His people. Whatever the case may be, the scope of covering all the possible rapture scenarios is too complex to expand upon in this one chapter. Just remember, whether the rapture is pretribulation, mid-tribulation, or post-tribulation, rest assured God has a plan and He is in control no matter what happens. The final outcome for those who participate in the rapture is unification with the Lord for eternity.

The second coming is the phase occurring at the end of the Tribulation, when things look completely hopeless. The end of the Tribulation will be a time of immense suffering as the antichrist rules over the world for the last 42 months of this period. God's wrath will also be released on the earth in the form of judgments, adding to the misery of humanity. I believe God will use these judgments in a last attempt effort to open the eyes of nonbelievers to see Jesus as their Savior. But without a doubt, these will be the worst catastrophes that have ever been witnessed in the history of mankind. The only solution to make this nightmare come to a conclusion is the return of Jesus.

In the second coming, Jesus will return to this world along with His army of the heavenly host. This return will mark the end of the Tribulation where the remaining people on the earth will proclaim war against the King. Jesus will appear riding a white horse striking down the opposing nations with a sharp two-edged sword from His mouth (Revelation 19:11–15), the Word of God. This last great battle called Armageddon will end in certain defeat for the ones who rally against Jesus. After this great victory, an angel will bind Satan and throw him into the bottomless pit where he will be bound for one thousand years (Revelation 20:2–3). The saints (believers) will rule and reign with Christ for a thousand years, a period known as the Millennium. Unbelievers who survived the Tribulation will also live during this time. These people will still have the ability to sin, but with the devil being bound, God's grace will reign, and a level of peace not experienced today will exist.

At the end of the Millennium, the devil will be released from the pit to stir up those who have a propensity to sin, rallying them to fight against the saints of God. God will send fire down from the heavens devouring the attackers, while all unbelievers will then be judged and condemned to eternal punishment. Satan will be thrown into the lake of fire, his permanent resting place where he can no longer cause havoc among the saints. A new heaven and earth will be created along with a glorious new city of Jerusalem where the righteous of God will live in eternal peace. The saints of God will be victorious through the power of Christ Jesus.

In the meantime, believers waiting on the second coming of Christ should be preparing themselves for His arrival. The ways of the world are counterintuitive to the ways of God and though Christians must live in the world, we should not partake in its practices. Preparation for His return should include the sanctification of our body, soul, and mind (1 Thessalonians 5:23). This means we should be submitting our entire being to the will of God while neglecting the ways of the world. God's ways are right, and any carnal belief is just a distraction to separate you from the truth. Sanctification of the body is to purpose it for godly service and not to perform acts of wickedness. Your soul should be in union with God until every fiber of your being is consumed with Him. The mind should be the gatekeeper of your brain, allowing it only to think good thoughts while stopping the entrance of all ungodly and evil ideas. Though we cannot complete all these mandates perfectly, we can repent and seek forgiveness when we fall short of the mark. So sweep your house clean and prepare it for the King!

This consecration of the spirit man will be an essential survival tool for end-time Christians. Jesus warned us in the final days there will be many false prophets and people who declare to be Christ (Matthew 24:24). They will display feats of supernatural power witnessing to their claim, but discernment must be applied to test their actions. Do they operate to appease the pleasure of the flesh or are these miracles in alignment with God's commandments? Do they glorify God with their works, or do they put the limelight on themselves? True disciples will always be configured with the will of God, bringing glory to Him and Him only. Jesus never pointed to Himself but always gave credit to the Father in anything He did. Using this philosophy, the followers of Christ will be easily able to identify the fakes. The counterfeit deity will not fool believers but will only strengthen a Christian's resolve knowing only something that is real can be falsely replicated. If there was no Christ, there would be no reason for the devil to produce a counterfeit substitute. So always cast your eyes upon Jesus, so you can tell the difference between the real thing and the imitation. The more time you spend in relationship with the Real Thing, the less likely you are to be deceived.

Many ask how we will know when we are approaching the end of times. The apostles considered this same question and asked Jesus what signs would mark His return. He replied there would be wars and rumors of wars, famines, pestilences, earthquakes, increased lawlessness; and the hearts of many would grow cold (Matthew 24:6–12). As we study the world arena, we can identify several confrontations that could erupt into major conflicts such as the tension in the Middle East with Israel, North Korean nuclear weapons development, and the Ukraine war to name a few. This fighting is aggravating the global food shortage along with the droughts and severe weather brought on by extreme climate changes. Pestilences, such as AIDS, SARS, Ebola, and the different strains of COVID have appeared in rapid succession causing much suffering and many deaths. Lawlessness is on the increase as many people become indifferent to the regular reports of mass shootings in the media. These seem like the birthing pains of the end days. I am not saying Jesus is going to return tomorrow, but when the contractions keep getting closer together, sooner rather than later, a baby will be born.

Jesus also warned that persecution of Christians will increase to include hatred so severe it will lead to death. In the United States, religious freedom is not associated with suffering, but more and more people are falling away from the faith. As this trend continues and more people adopt the philosophy of the world culture, a force in direct opposition to the doctrine of God will generate future tensions. People in other countries outside of the U.S. are already paying a heavy price for their belief in Christ. Some are being disowned by their families, while others experience persecution and yes, even death. No matter what the outcome is, hold firm to the end for the Lord God is with you.

All these end-time characteristics are designed to cause an atmosphere of fear and chaos. Only those who abide in Christ will be absent of fear, for fear is a spirit generated from evil. The King of days, the Lord Jesus Christ, has given us the courage to advance in this end-time scenario and we are to proceed to the battlefield with the mindset of victory. When God is for you, the enemy will surely be defeated. Besides, there is no need to worry because even Jesus said, "I am coming quickly" (Revelation 22:20).

CHAPTER 22

The Homecoming

When believers are called up into the air to meet Jesus, there will be a great celebration in heaven. This event is called the marriage supper of the Lamb and it will commemorate the spiritual joining of the Church to the Lord Jesus Christ. Blessed are those who are called to the marriage supper of the Lamb (Revelation 19:9). This will be the feast of all feasts and the party will surpass any expectation we could now conceive. The glory of God will surround all Christians and the pain and suffering we experience here in this life will exist no more. The church will be filled with joy and peace that it never could have dreamed of.

Preparations have already been made for the children of God when they enter heaven. Jesus said, "In My Father's house there are many mansions and I go to prepare a place for you" (John 14:2). The King of kings has prepared a place especially for you and He is sitting in heaven enthusiastically waiting for your arrival. What a glorious day it will be for His faithful servants. This gift is extended to all people who believe in the Lord Jesus Christ. This life and world will pass away, but the new heaven and earth will last forever. An eternity with God costs you nothing because Jesus has already paid the price. Come enjoy the fruits of His sacrifice!

At the end of this age, we will once again return to the garden-like state where we will fellowship with God for eternity. Everything will have come full circle as believers return to God's rest the way it was intended to be. No longer will the devil be able to torment you and cause havoc in your spirit, for God will have taken care of Satan once and for all. It saddens me to think some people will not receive the gift Jesus wants them so desperately to have. An eternity in hell is an excruciating punishment I would not wish on anybody. I pray that all nonbelievers reading this book will be convicted by the Holy Spirit and turn their lives over to Jesus. Jesus is the only way to eternal life in heaven.

Some people have asked me, "What if you are wrong and heaven does not exist?" The answer I give them is if heaven did not exist, I would still live a life that honors God. If I live God's way, I will have lived a life serving others and being the best person I possibly can be. In addition, I will probably be remembered fondly by the people I have touched. That does not seem like a bad legacy to me. Then the question I ask them is, "What if heaven does exist and you miss your chance to experience it?" From a Christian perspective, it is a win/win situation even if heaven did not exist, but from a nonbeliever's standpoint, there is a great downside. The prophecies in the Bible have been fulfilled with astounding accuracy, so I am not going to bet against the Bible and what it says about heaven. The Bible is God's inspired word and you have to remember God does not lie, so heaven has to be real.

If you do not already know the Lord, I hope this book has convinced you to make a decision to live for Christ. It is God's wish for no one to perish, which is why He allowed His only Son to suffer and die so you can be saved. If you are already a Christian, I hope this book has encouraged you to keep fighting the good fight, while giving you a better understanding of Christianity. Satan is out and about trying to rock your boat, but do not be afraid to step out of your comfort zone and confront the waves. With God on your side, surely victory is within your grasp. I am looking forward to spending an eternity with you in the presence of our God, the Lord Jesus Christ. Greetings until then and keep on serving a now God!

ABOUT THE AUTHOR

Pete Martin is a minister, professor, and engineer who was radically saved at age of forty-two. The author is an avid believer in the power of the Holy Spirit, using the gifts to reach the lost and encourage new Christians. Pete resides in the state of South Carolina with his wife Kim.

Printed in the USA
CPSIA information can be obtained
at www.ICGtesting.com
LVHW041939100424
776966LV00003B/505

9 798888 516140